GREETINGS FROM CANADA

TO THE EDWARDIANS
whose enthusiasm for postcards
and whose chatty messages
endowed us with this engrossing portrait
of turn-of-the-century Canada

The Post Card Girl (Copyright)

ALLAN ANDERSON BETTY TOMLINSON

GREETINGS FROM CANADA

An Album of Unique Canadian Postcards from the Edwardian Era 1900-1916

Macmillan of Canada TORONTO

PRIVATE POST CARD

PLACE
POSTAGE STAMP
HERE

This space may be used for Correspondence

This space is exclusively for the Address

Canadian Cataloguing in Publication Data

Anderson, Allan, 1915-
Greetings from Canada

ISBN 0-7705-1736-6 bd. ISBN 0-7705-1721-8 pa.

1. Canada—Description and travel—1900-1950—Views.* 2. Postal cards—Canada. I. Tomlinson, Betty, 1923- II. Title.

FC59.A54 917.1'00222 C78-001532-0
F1015.A54

The Macmillan Company of Canada Limited
70 Bond Street, Toronto
Ontario M5B 1X3

It was 1904 when I got my first postcard, it came from Moose Jaw. Well, from then on we all seemed to get cards from our relatives and friends. After some time, a very appropriate Christmas gift was a postcard album. I was thrilled with mine, and every card that came, I couldn't get to the postcard album quick enough to put it in place.

You would keep your album in the parlour in those days, and when people came to visit you had to show your collection first thing. Everybody was interested in it. You might fill two albums and then you'd start putting them in boxes.

I bought cards, too, to send to my friends. Even our local drugstore sold cards of our town—all kinds of scenes—and we were anxious to send them back East to show just what our prairie town looked like.

I must have had 800 cards or more. Practically all the young people collected cards, that was the thing to do. There was a real fad for collecting in those days. . . .

MONA WOOD
Pense, Saskatchewan

Souvenir
PostCard
PLACE A
ONE CENT
POSTAGE STAMP
HERE
BEFORE
MAILING
COPYRIGHT 1904
W·M·WAITE
POST
CARD
STAMP
HERE
This Space may be used for Correspondence
This Space for Address Only
Atkinson Bros., Publishers, Toronto.

Contents

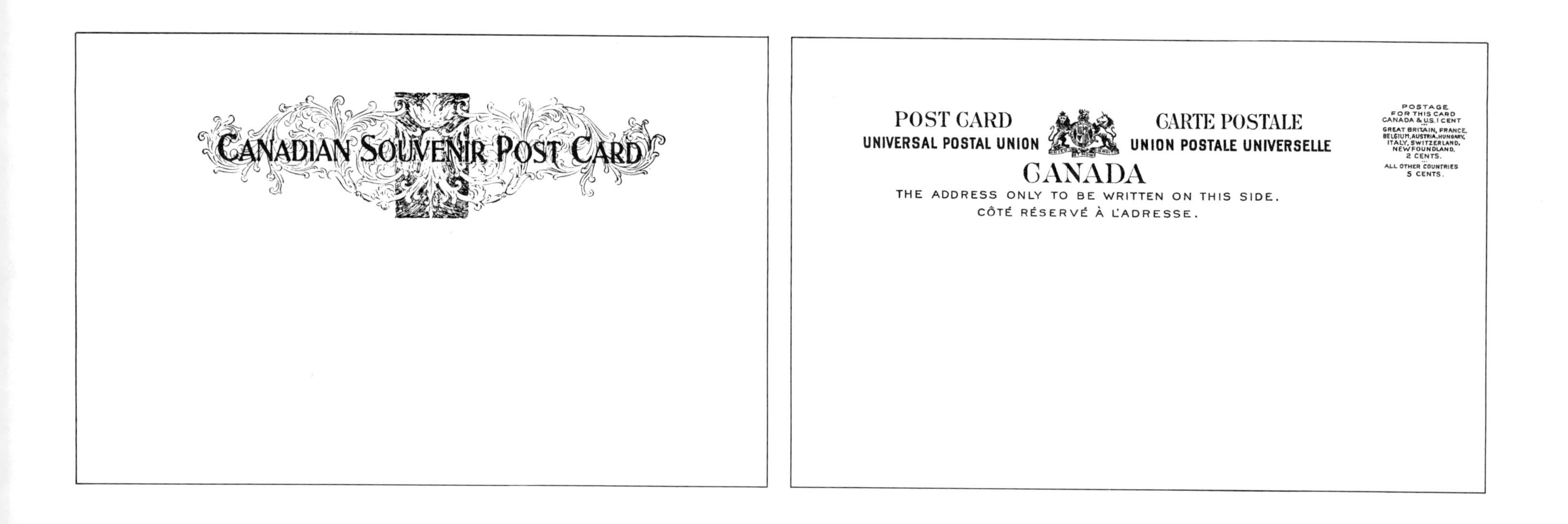
CANADIAN SOUVENIR POST CARD
POST CARD
UNIVERSAL POSTAL UNION
CARTE POSTALE
UNION POSTALE UNIVERSELLE
CANADA
THE ADDRESS ONLY TO BE WRITTEN ON THIS SIDE.
CÔTÉ RÉSERVÉ À L'ADRESSE.
POSTAGE
FOR THIS CARD
CANADA & U.S. 1 CENT
GREAT BRITAIN, FRANCE,
BELGIUM, AUSTRIA, HUNGARY,
ITALY, SWITZERLAND,
NEWFOUNDLAND,
2 CENTS.
ALL OTHER COUNTRIES
5 CENTS.

Acknowledgements

In the passionate search for additions to our postcard collection, many kind people have given generously of their time and resources. As authors are forever saying, we "can only name a few of them."

At the outset, George Jackson of Milton, Ontario, and Charlie Lamont of Burlington traded cards with us while offering much needed help and advice. Gordon Ribble of Oakville was a kind friend who sold us many very good cards and who waited patiently, sometimes for long periods, to be paid. So, too, did Eleanor and Jack Norris of Kitchener, who became good friends. We have spent long days going through postcards at their home, selecting hundreds at a time.

Ruth Keiver of Three Hills, Alberta, sent a carton full of postcard albums—among the best cards we have ever seen—and we can't thank her enough for this magnificent gift. Clare Willis of Oakville also uncovered some excellent cards on two occasions. Mona Wood of Pense, Saskatchewan, not only provided us with the finest cards of a small town, but wrote cheerful notes about Pense in the old days, and about her memories of collecting cards in Edwardian times. A handful of postcards in this book were lent to us by other collectors and we thank them for their courtesy.

Pat Rogal of the Toronto Public Library and Ron D'Altroy of the Vancouver Public Library willingly helped us at various times, and we thank them both.

Rena Krawagna of the CBC was enthusiastic about these postcards from the first day she saw them, and through her commissioning of twenty-six postcard themes to be used on CBC-TV, badly needed financial support was guaranteed. Film Arts of Toronto put together these little films and we express our gratitude to Don Haig, John Griffin, and Don Evraire for the creative skill which made these films so very beautiful.

There is no adequate way to thank Ken Bagnell, editor of the *Imperial Oil Review*. Not only did he start a snowball rolling with an article he commissioned on the postcards but, on behalf of Imperial Oil, he made available to this project reproductions of old postcards which originally appeared in the *Review*. To Ken Bagnell and Imperial Oil: your generosity is greatly appreciated.

Dick Cole, one of the ablest photographers in the country, did a remarkable job of photographing in black-and-white some of the coloured cards in the collection. Rick Miller, Art Director at Macmillan of Canada, has contributed his expertise, enthusiasm, and sensitivity to the physical preparation of this volume.

Most of all, we want to mention Jan Walter, our editor at Macmillan, who was always patient with us, and who invariably knew what was right for the book.

With 35,000 Edwardian cards to select from and a great mass of material to digest, it has not been an easy task, but it has been an act of total devotion for us. Edwardian Canada deserves our love, and has it.

ALLAN ANDERSON
BETTY TOMLINSON
Tottenham, Ontario
July 31, 1978

TUCK'S POST CARD

CARTE POSTALE. POSTKARTE.

(For Address Only.)

By Appointment.

The Peter Redpath Museum contains large and valuable collections in botany, zoology, mineralogy and geology, arranged in such a manner as to facilitate the work in these departments.

McGILL UNIVERSITY, MONTREAL.

Raphael Tuck & Sons' "OILETTE" Postcard 2688

ART PUBLISHERS TO THEIR MAJESTIES THE KING & QUEEN

Miss S. K. Martin,
2146 - First Ave West
Vancouver
B.C.

Printed in England.

POST CARD
FAMOUS THROUGHOUT THE WORLD.

Address Only.

The Valentine & Sons' Publishing Co., Ltd. Montreal
Printed in Great Britain

Hoping you will like all, & that I will hear from you again soon I remain.
Yours very sincerely
Percy C. Casey

P.S. Please note that my address is once again changed.

B. Horn, Esq.
Toronto.

Introduction

THE YEARS FROM THE TURN OF THE CENTURY to the First World War were good ones for Canada, and the nation and its citizenry made the most of that brief, but glorious era. To many of us Edwardian Canada seems endless years ago, yet it was the age of our parents and grandparents, and of course, there are Edwardians still with us who embody that sprightliness of mind, that psychic energy, which are hallmarks of the Edwardians. Men and women alike displayed a characteristic flair, a cheerful buoyancy, and a breezy optimism. Family ties and strong friendships were held dear, yet there existed an independence of spirit that encouraged a certain brashness, even audacity.

The Edwardian picture postcard was made to order for the Edwardian personality. Plain old-fashioned gab came easily to them, and, with frequent and efficient mail delivery, the postcard performed the same function as the modern-day telephone. The messages possess all the conversation, gossip, frank opinions, and everyday trivia of the party line, and Edwardians became worried and annoyed when their friends or relatives failed to write regularly. To the researcher who seeks the true flavour of the age, these outspoken and detailed messages offer an incomparable, first-hand social history of the period.

A good place to begin an examination of the Edwardians is right at home, with my own ancestors. Though perhaps somewhat unusual, on balance they do represent the age. My maternal grandfather had a jewellery business in Owen Sound, Ontario, which he lost eventually because, being a sensible man, he much preferred sailing on Georgian Bay to minding the store. Like grandfather, the Edwardians loved the outdoors and active sports of all kinds.

This grandfather had a brother who flatly refused to do a day's work in his life, his sole preoccupation being a second-rate racehorse. Likewise, the Edwardians could display quirky streaks—they weren't as easily whipped into line as were the two generations that followed them.

Grandfather had another brother who abandoned his bride after only a month of married life and went off to the Rockies to paint, never, as far as we know, to be seen in the East again. I have one of his paintings and certainly he had talent, but wanderlust dominated him as much as art. The same passion for travel affected the Edwardians generally, though less dramatically. Trains went everywhere, fares were low, and everyone had family or acquaintances to visit.

Father, who married mother in Owen Sound, was the other side of the Edwardian coin. Invariably he retired no later than eleven o'clock at night and every morning he rose at seven. He ate his porridge in the time-honoured fashion, dipping each spoonful in cream the way his Scottish forebears had done. He worked forty-four years for the CPR, and once went thirteen years without taking a holiday. Possessed of a kindly disposition and universally well-liked, he was the finest gentleman I have ever known. Like him, the Edwardians worked very hard, though most resented the desperately long hours that were demanded of them.

And let us not be fooled by the façade of dress — all those straw hats, bowlers, and stiff collars on the men, the petticoats and flowing gowns on the women. These may make the age seem stiff and formal, but, in fact, it was a relaxed, extroverted, lively time. This, in spite of the fact that there was great social inequality. The poor, especially immigrants, huddled in squalid hovels in the large cities, while some of the wealthy were outrageously rich, snatching all they could lay their hands on with no income tax to worry about.

The Edwardian period has often been referred to as the Glorious Age of the Picture Postcard, but the popularity of the cards extended beyond the reign of Edward VII and stocks lingered in stores until 1916. They depicted every corner of Canada from Newfoundland to the Yukon and every facet of life, rural or urban.

This particular book would not exist had I not had the good luck, six years ago, to stumble on a packet of early cards at the home of a rare book dealer. Two weeks later, I found a large-sized and utterly charming card of the port of St. John's, Newfoundland, which is reproduced in these pages. I have always had a consuming passion for Canadian history, and the fact that I could lay my hands on a visual approach to it excited me immensely. Fortunately, in those days, I travelled all over Canada preparing radio documentaries for the CBC, and had many opportunities to scrounge through antique stores, discover the few genuine postcard dealers in Canada, and zealously track down polite ladies in their eighties who were willing to sell whole albums of Edwardian cards for modest sums.

I bought all the cards that interested me—cards postmarked from 1899 to 1916. Postdated cheques were scattered across the country; fortunately, dealers have almost unlimited patience with the true, ardent collector, and eventually all the bills were paid. Today Betty and I jointly own a collection that exceeds 35,000 cards. It would be impossible to purchase the majority of these cards now, and some indeed are much more expensive than they used to be.

Reading the messages on the cards, it became clear that we had at our fingertips an unparalleled panorama of Edwardian times. Most people did not save letters, but postcards were eagerly and lovingly placed in decorative albums and kept in the parlour. It was obligatory that friends and visitors view the album and admire new acquisitions.

It is commonly acknowledged that the picture postcard was invented in Austria in 1869. Before the turn of the century there were postcards, highly decorative and with an arrangement of pictures on the front, circulating on the Continent. By and large, however, government post offices retained a monopoly on the issuance of postcards, in the main prestamped cards with a plain back. They were used widely for business messages. When this monopoly was lifted at or before the new century, manufacturers, who had already honed their skills to a fine point with coloured printed material of other kinds, turned to the production of postcards with extraordinary results.

J. V. Valentine and Sons of Dundee, Scotland, produced by far the most beautiful view cards. Tuck's of England were excellent also. Valentine's turned out 20,000 Canadian views, although the first 12,000 are the best. They numbered their Canadian cards from 100,000 to 120,000, and the first turned up in Canada, so we understand, about 1906. There were some six or seven Canadian manufacturers who counted; Warwick Bro's & Rutter of Toronto was the leading producer. The large manufacturers, British and Canadian, produced thousands of cards in colour. The British companies sometimes sent out their own representatives to photograph Canadian scenes. Originally black and white, the photographs were exquisitely hand-coloured and lithographed, usually in Germany. Almost from the beginning the quality of the cards was fantastic, but it all came to an end with the First World War although, as mentioned earlier, the stores carried stock until about 1916. That year is the last postmarked date of the majority of Edwardian cards.

Not to be forgotten are uncounted village and town photographers who did black-and-white photocards, often of superb quality. These ambitious professionals climbed watertowers and church steeples to take bird's-eye views of their communities, or snapped trains at stations, or recorded the aftermath of disasters, or turned their cameras on little side streets and clicked away. Nothing was considered too mundane or insignificant.

What is of greatest value is that these photographers had a fine sense of the immediacy of events and the interest of daily life. They caught in the cards the movement and involvement of people in everyday activities, on the streets, at parks, beaches, or markets—all the immense variety of themes displayed in this book. And variety there was. As far as is known today, there were 1,600 *different* views of Edwardian Toronto, 1,250 of Ottawa, 600 of Peterborough, and 150 of Bobcaygeon, Ontario.

Who were these busy photographers? We know some of them: Bald of Owen Sound, Herrington of Trenton, ("180,000 Photo Post Cards made in 1912"), Marcell, who took vivid action shots of the first Calgary Stampede in 1912 and the Winnipeg Stampede of 1913, and a natty little Englishman, Chapman of Victoria. Each of them covered a fairly wide area around his home base and there were hundreds of unknowns.

About 1902-03 it became a fad in Canada among well-to-do women to collect postcards in albums. The hobby caught on with all kinds of people and became a craze, spawning postcard clubs and exchanges across the country. The post office, which in those days believed not only in delivering the mail but in delivering it promptly, kept a record of the number of postcards Canadians sent. As early as 1900, Canadians posted over 27,000 cards. In 1908, 41,000,000 cards were mailed, and in 1913, well over 60,000,000. Remember, the population of Canada in 1901 was 5,371,315 and in 1911, 7,206,643.

The cards were known as "postals". Over and over, messages began: "Got your pretty postal." These early postcards gave Canadians a visual sense of the country unlike anything they had had before. It is not too much to say that postals linked the country together and that they contributed significantly to a sense of Canadian identity. This message is dated 1909 and was sent from Halifax across Canada to Chemainus, B.C., near Nanaimo: "I have nearly 2,000 cards. I collect cards of schools and colleges. Could you send me cards like that as I would like ever so much to see what your colleges are like. As ever, Effie."

Two collectors who keep popping up in our cards, and who seem to have driven themselves into a frenzy with the volume of their correspondence, are P. E. Cavey of Winnipeg and Baker Horn of Toronto. This is Cavey to Horn in February 1912, early in their postal acquaintanceship: "Dear Friend—Many thanks for your pretty P.C. just received. Yes, I enjoy P.C. exchanging very much as through it I have got to know some splendid fellows. I have nearly 1000 cards. I have been here over two years, having come from Jersey, Channel Islands, near France, originally. Winnipeg is a grand city & is, I think, much finer than Toronto. No, I do not collect stamps now, I gave it up long ago. With kind regards. P. E. Cavey." On a later card and in a somewhat disgruntled manner (or maybe it's just jealousy), Cavey says: "How on earth do you manage to write to so many P.C. people? I have between 40-50 regular exchanges & it keeps me going to write to those!"

Horn, who always stamped his cards "Baker Horn Post Card Exchange and Stamp Collector," was, in fact, at the breaking point. In this message, he knocks off one collector: "Dear Chum—Thanks for cards received and I regret to say I must cease correspondence with you as I have so many friends writing that I am cutting out some of them as it is impossible to keep them all up, but I am sending you the name of another chum who is anxious to correspond and sends good cards." One pictures poor old Horn, scribbling away on postals half the night and going in to work the next morning, red-eyed and ratty from lack of sleep and nervous exhaustion.

Among the most exotic messages are those on some 120 cards, all in mint condition, that show mainly views of Montreal. A woman in that city began sending cards to a man in a mid-western American town; apparently they were members of the same postcard exchange. Between 1911 and 1912 she covered the backs of dozens of cards, sending six to twelve at a time and always enclosing them in an envelope. The longer the correspondence continued, the more torrid the messages became, yet it was purely a disembodied affair. As far as we know they never met.

Time has glossed over this long-forgotten romance, and we have none of his cards to her, but the passion of her ardour is evident still.

Dear Friend—I really was more than pleased at receiving your last photo. You can be sure also I will not let it get cold. If you keep my photos in front of your writing desk, be careful I do not pull my hand out and have you make blotters on your correspondence. How would you like that? I think I will be so busy with you that I will not have time to write my friends. As ever, Louise.

My dear Friend—Your lovely cards received. I am sure you did guess what I did to that pretty face of yours, but wish me to tell you. Very well, I took the photo, gave it a hearty kiss, and asked a few questions, but you did not answer. I have no doubt it would be sweeter if I kissed you instead of your photo, but you are so far it is impossible. Now, dear, I will close for this time hoping you and yours are in the best of health. Do not forget that I will be in Dreamland at 11 P.M. tonight, so come, Dear. With best wishes, love and kisses. As ever I remain your friend, Louise.

My dearest Friend—At last I will answer your very pretty cards. When C. is home it is impossible for me to answer any of my mail as he always wants me to tell him what I am writing. Yes, dear, if it had been the original, instead of the photo, he would have got more than one kiss. I know on my side it will be much sweeter to kiss you than your photo. If my photo is so near your bed, I wish I could come out of it when you are asleep. I would do more than tease you then. Your naughty friend, Louise.

Nowhere is the history of Canada brought more triumphantly alive than on early postcards from homesteaders in the West. Before the turn of the century the West was virgin prairie. Edward Blake, who had been leader of the Liberal party, spoke in 1891 of "an empty West, empty still". *The Times* of Winnipeg lamented that "the trails from Manitoba to the States were worn bare and barren by the footprints of departing settlers". In 1896, only 902 immigrants applied for homesteads, and, deducting the homesteaders who gave up, the total figure for immigrants and Canadians who sought homesteads that year was a meagre 1,400. Then Clifford Sifton stepped into Laurier's cabinet in 1896 and became Minister of the Interior.

Sifton had previously castigated the Department saying, "The crying complaint was that it was a department of delay, a department of circumlocution, a department in which people could not get business done, a department which tired men to death who undertook to get any business transacted with it." Sifton turned all that around. Aggressively, he sought immigrants in the United States, the United Kingdom, and Europe. Some people began howling about foreigners pouring into the country, but Sifton countered with the now famous statement: "I think a stalwart peasant in a sheep-skin coat, born on the soil, whose forefathers have been farmers for ten generations, with a stout wife and a half-dozen children, is good quality."

Though Sifton left the Cabinet in 1905 after a disagreement with Laurier, his policies prevailed and a flood of immigrants poured into the West. According to the Canada Year Book 1913, the rate of increase of population in Canada between 1901 and 1911 was the greatest in the world—34.17 per cent. Saskatchewan's population in that decade jumped a phenomenal 439 per cent, and Alberta's 413 per cent, though each was still under the half-million mark. The greatest year for immigration was 1913, when 402,432 people arrived in Canada, almost as many from the United States as from the United Kingdom, and a somewhat smaller number from other countries.

Many eastern Canadians left the relative security of Ontario farms and lined up in the West for homesteads. Here is a message, dated August 20, 1910, and written on five postcards, that tells of one man's experience:

My dearest Friend—Well, here I am in Regina again. I suppose you will begin to think I am nearly living here, but I am not, for this is the last time I am coming down until Christmas, or just before. This is twice for me this week but I was on very important business. I was after a homestead and I got it, too. It is a dandy and only twelve miles from Craik and five miles from a nice town called Liberty on the CPR. *I have not got to go on it until next February but I am going on in November and stay all winter.*

You will have to excuse scribbling as I am nearly asleep. I didn't get in until half-past two this morning and didn't go to bed at all. I was at the land office at half-past five this morning and waited there until nine. You know the first one there has the first chance and that homestead I got would have been filed on a dozen times since nine if it was open yet, but it just opened today and I got it.

I am taking music lessons now, learning to play a mandolin. I can play quite a bit on it already. That is all I will have to do this winter, just sit in the shack and play while I am holding down the homestead.

Now, Nellie, you want to be a good true little girl to your little boy in the West. I will have to ring off as this is the last of this set of cards. I remain, Your ever true love, W. J. B.

There is a kind of tough exuberance in many of the messages from the prairies. This one, for instance, was sent to Strathburn, Ontario: "Dear Stanley—This is from the West, the land of Snow, Frost, and Wind, Heat, Sunshine, and Dust, Wheat, Oats, and Barley. Yours, Jack."

The Edwardians were acutely aware of nature in a way that we are not. Expressions of delight in the beauty of the natural world are invariably simple and straightforward, and not at all prosy or affected. Bill Marshall, a friend and antique dealer at Deux Montagnes, Quebec, describes it thus:

The Edwardians saw their world differently. They lived a larger percentage of their time out-of-doors. Their eyes were adjusted for a 180-degree vision of the world, whereas the television screen is bringing us down to something like a 30-degree vision of the world. I see them enjoying a sunset to a much greater degree than we would—the woods in early spring, the springs coming alive again after being frozen: they could see things like this, they could hear them. The sound of dripping water wasn't drowned by the din of a nearby auto route.

Often people simply worried about crops or announced that the potatoes and turnips or wheat and oats were doing well. But the appreciation of nature was there, especially in lyrical and literate comments such as these messages sent from Victoria in September and October 1906. The writer is obviously an Englishwoman.

The country roads here remind us very much of the Home ones, with their bracken, bramble & hips at either side. Oaks are characteristic of this district but most of the trees, of all kinds, are very weather-beaten. . . . We walk as far as some steps leading down to the beach . . . just below that there are salmon nets. The view, looking across the Straits of Juan de Fuca to the Olympic Range on the American side, is simply beautiful. A good many big steamers pass & lots of smaller boats & canoes. We often see the "Princess Victoria," coming in from Vancouver, & she makes great waves break on the shore. The canoes are so quaint & picturesque & lend a great charm to the view, especially at sunset—the Indians go out fishing in them & often sing as they paddle along. Some of them (Indians, not canoes!) wear large straw hats. Yesterday the sunset on the Straits was most beautiful & one Indian in his canoe "crossed the pathway of the sun"—it was quite Hiawathian*! We are having the Indian summer & the sea-air is delicious. Ina.*

It was a halcyon period but it is no contradiction to say that it inflicted its share of hardships. Illness plagued Canadians; it is almost impossible to imagine the range and extent of diseases until one browses through these old cards. Here's a sample litany of woe:

Lake of Bays, Ont., July 4, 1909: Sophia has bronchitis & measles. I am the only one that can look after her night or day. I am getting tired of it now but I have more of it yet.

Berwick, N.S., 1911: They are having a bad time with diphtheria around Berwick. They must be getting alarmed having closed the schools and churches.

Thornhill, Ont., June 14, 1909: The kiddies have all had the measles & Birdie New Ammonia [sic] *and the mumps too.*

Revelstoke, B.C., April 22, 1911: I got back to Revelstoke and just nicely got started to work when I burnt my neck with a red-hot coal. Got my neck pretty well doctored up and I got the mumps and German measles. Well, I thought sure I was getting on the sick list steady but if I don't get anything else I think I'll be able to go to work about the 24th.

This foreboding message was sent from Welland, Ont.: "Congratulate your mother upon getting through the winter so well when so many have been called away. Surely our turn is not far distant and how important that we be ready, for the messenger may come in an hour we think not."

On the back of a card showing St. Paul's Hospital, Vancouver: "Only $10 per day in here. Thank Goodness I ain't ill often."

Accidents could be equally catastrophic. This is a singular reference to an automobile mishap: Toronto, Ont., January 28, 1906: "The young fellow who admired Grace's picture is dying. He was struck by a car last Monday and his skull is split."

Another message is a virtual catalogue of misfortune, yet at this distance it seems almost hilarious:

Okanagan Landing, B.C.: Ray and Carrie are so tired they sleep till 8 A.M. Very hot and dry and dusty here. Will stuck a nail head first in the ball of his great toe and made a bad wound. Laid up three days for it and is still very lame. Carrie broke her collar-bone, Ray cut his knee, and I sprained my ankle. One cow has a calf, one has a sore leg and the cat has kittens under the house where the hens have chickens. Trouble, trouble, trouble.

Postcards were the vehicle for many a shameless flirt, and in matters of the heart Edwardians were outspoken. Here they are in full flight on a card from Oakville, Ont.: "There are several parks in town besides this. It is a very nice place to spoon in the evenings. Jack."

From Pearl in Winnipeg, Man., to Frank in Moose Jaw, Sask., August 29, 1907: "Well, Frank, I guess you will think I am a dandy at answering Post Cards but here goes. What are you doing with yourself anyhow? Suppose you have a nice little girl up there and have become completely *infatuated*. . . ."

Paris, Ont., July 6, 1907: "Dear Friend Ira—Don't think I am sore but you needn't write to me any more for you can't keep two on a string, I want you to understand. I am very sorry I sent you those last three cards for what I have heard. I don't go behind your back to tell you, like you have done. Well, good bye. Nellie."

From Toronto, Ont., to Niagara Falls: "True to my promise I am having a fine time. If any more soldiers come to the Falls hold them till I come."

From Wilton, Ont., to Yarker, July 30, 1909: "Hello, Nellie—got back from camp safe and sound and when I got home there stood before my eyes a new buggy and if you will be at home next Sunday I will be out and give you a drive, between 6:30 and 7 o'clock."

From Strathroy, Ont., to Consecon, February 8, 1909: "I hear that Mr. S. is going to be married soon. What do you girls mean by letting him slip through your fingers? Annie."

From Bloomfield, N.S., to Kingsport: "Can't you get anyone better than a married man?"

From Moose Jaw, Sask.: "Dear Bertha—It is awful lonesome and dull—no weddings. The girls are all past redemption here as far as weddings go. Eleanor."

And finally, this irresistible plea: "Sweetheart—I will be heart-broken if I don't get to see you tonight. The boss will not be home until 10 P.M."

Canadians passed the time on trains by scribbling postcards to friends all across the country. This is our favourite train message: "Dear Peg—This will be posted later but I thought I could write a letter on a stiff card. The train shakes very much and Ethel seems quite seasick. I gave her a dose of brandy which has done her good as she is now buried in her book." Ethel was buried in her book, no doubt about it—sleeping it off.

Literate and perceptive English journalists made it a habit in those years to visit Canada and report on it, sometimes enthusiastically, sometimes critically. R. E. Vernede, a colourful English writer, wrote a fascinating account of Canada titled *The Fair Dominion—A Record of Canadian Impressions*, published in 1911. Travel books were very popular in those days and Canada a desirable target, though usually we come off very well in such books. We start with Vernede in Montreal:

Montreal has, so I am told, sixty-four millionaires—real, not dollar millionaires; self-made, not descended millionaires; strenuous, not idle millionaires. Most of them live in Sherbrooke Street, or near it, on the way up to the Mountain. It is a fine wide road with an extraordinary variety of houses in it. You cannot point to any one house and say this is the sort of house a millionaire builds, for the next one is quite different, and so is the next and the next. It is natural that Canadians should be more original in their house-building than our millionaires. They are more original men altogether.

The more is the pity that there should be slums. Why does Montreal possess them? Largely, I suppose, for the reason that any very great city possesses them. There are landlords who can make money out of them, there are people so poor that they will live in them; and their poverty is accounted for by the fact that cities draw the destitute as the moon the tides.

The English poet Rupert Brooke saw Toronto in 1913. This is from his *Letters from America*:

Toronto (pronounce T'ranto, please) is difficult to describe. It has an individuality, but an elusive one; yet not through any queerness or difficult shade of eccentricity; a subtly normal, an indefinably obvious personality. It is a healthy, cheerful city (by modern standards); a clean-shaven, pink-faced, respectably dressed, fairly energetic, unintellectual, passably sociable, well-to-do, public-school-and-varsity sort of city.

This is Vernede's assessment of Torontonians, and his impressions of Winnipeg, Calgary and Victoria:

I will only say that if you can imagine a Lowland Scot, cautious and self-possessed, outwardly resisting American exuberance and extravagance, but inwardly by slow degrees absorbing—and thereby moderating—that hustling spirit of which these things are manifestations, you have something not unlike the Canadian of Toronto.

* * * *

Winnipeg, instead of consisting of elevators and all the apparatus connected with the storage of wheat, was all banks and cinematograph parlours. There were, it is true, shops and such things sandwiched in between. I recall a jeweller's shop containing the suitable and attractive placard in its window—"Marriage Licences for Sale Here." It is true, too, that banks and cinematograph shows are not unconnected with wheat. In the banks you store the dollars you have made out of wheat; at the cinematograph shows you circulate them. But really there was an almost incredible number of these institutions.

Of the two kinds of business I felt that personally I would rather own a moving picture show. Winnipegers are, I feel sure, easy to amuse. And they look exceedingly prosperous. The air of prosperity struck me as more obvious in Winnipeg than in any other part of Canada.

* * * *

A few years ago Calgary had no future to speak of. Men not as yet middle-aged can remember camping in Calgary in tents. There was only one place to dance in, and ranchers used to take turns at entering it. Now Calgary is a stone-built town of solid appearance, and still more solid importance. Like so many other Canadian towns, it is more important than it looks. It looks bustling enough, but hardly important. There are no buildings of a size to take the eye. The hotels are singularly inadequate. They are not only not comfortable enough for their guests, but they are not large enough. I had occasion to visit Calgary twice within a week, and each time I got the last bed in a different hotel, and tried to be thankful for it, but did not succeed.

* * * *

I was on the steamboat, ready to start for Vancouver, when the great fire of 1910 broke out in the town. With a considerable wind blowing it seemed to me not improbable that the whole of Victoria would be burnt down that night, and I had sufficient of the journalistic instinct to leave my things to go on by the boat and to go back myself to watch the blaze. Luckily the wind dropped and the fire was kept to one quarter, and I rather regretted my haste when I found myself stranded in Victoria at three o'clock in the morning. Still, it was worth while to have been there, if only to observe the working of the Canadian mind in a crisis of this sort. In England you would have heard ejaculations of horror and much sympathy expressed with those who were bound to suffer by the fire. The Victorian crowd took it quite differently. "This'll create more work," said one man fervidly. "Just what the town needed," said another enthusiast. "We'll be able to have a better-looking street there after this. Those shops weren't good enough." I even heard some of the men who had rushed out of their burning offices talking keenly and proudly of the sort of buildings they'd have to start putting up next day—much better buildings. Presumably they were insured, but even so men in the old country would have been a little shocked and perturbed, and regretful of the old rooms they were accustomed to. I fell asleep, when I had found a hotel, almost oppressed by the optimism of Canada.

Such was Edwardian Canada in the minds of British visitors. Their comments catch the energy, the bustle, the get-it-done spirit of the country. Obviously its citizens were friendly and gregarious and they radiated optimism. John Hobson, the English writer, coined the expression "the twentieth century belongs to Canada", and most Canadians would have agreed with him. Immigration pamphlets declared Canada "the land of opportunity", and that it was.

The Edwardian era was a brief, golden summer before the catastrophe of the First World War, an age of naiveté that will never come again. This book is not intended to serve as a definitive study; rather, it is a casual, over-the-fence encounter with an era about which Canadians know very little. Its purpose is to deal in human terms with history—not as a dry remnant of the past, but as a vibrant source of inspiration that should enliven and inform the present. No better medium could be found than these early picture postcards and their animated messages, as fresh as if they were written yesterday.

ALLAN ANDERSON

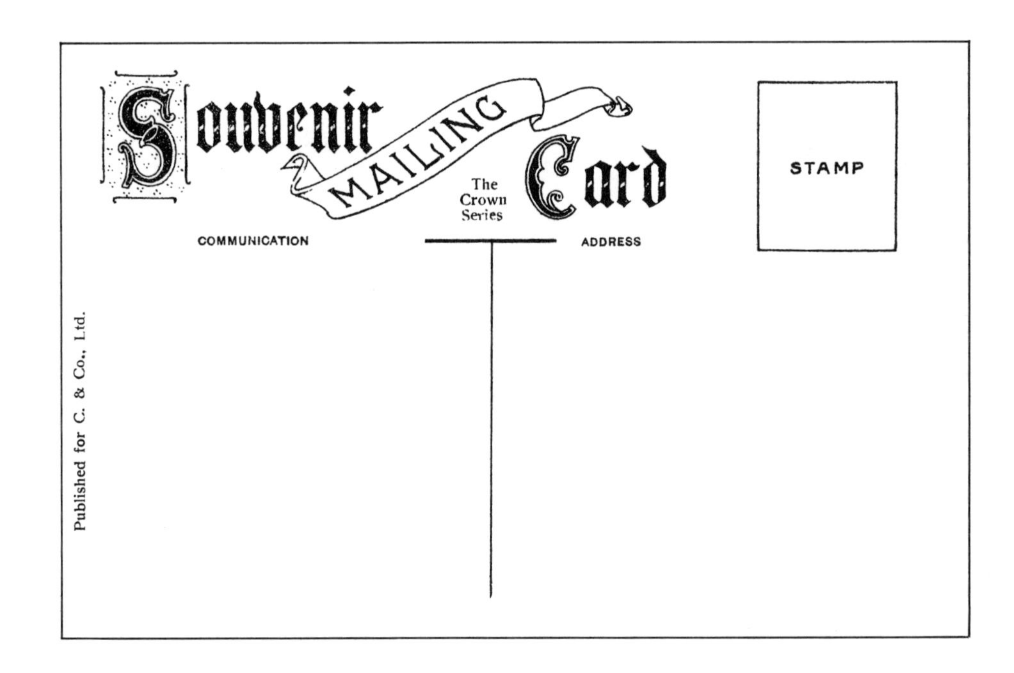
Souvenir
MAILING
Card
The Crown Series
STAMP
COMMUNICATION
ADDRESS
Published for C. & Co., Ltd.

Towns & Villages

THE VILLAGES OF EDWARDIAN CANADA were sleepy, dreamy little places, and we freely admit to romanticizing them. Villagers and townspeople enjoyed busy, gossipy lives; everyone knew and noticed everyone else. The Edwardians couldn't stand being lost in the crowd—that was not for them. A young man from Kingston visited Warkworth, Ontario, a not inconsiderable village, and wrote a complaining card to his girl at home: "Hello Birdy—I am not having a good time here at all. I feel like a cent and a half. This town is worse than a graveyard."

Still they could be light-hearted about it. On the back of a picture of a cemetery in Aurora, this message: "Dear Sylvia—Have got to stay here another week, wish I had a hobble skirt or could do something desperate, it's the limit. There must be all of one light for the town but I am really enjoying it. Expect to be home next Monday."

A final put down—and how well they could express themselves: "Dear Mac—Put this card to your ear, if you hear any sound you will hear more than you would if you were here." Some of the messages are pleasantly breezy: September 27, 1915, Valleyfield, Que.: "This is not a very picturesque burg but you can have a good time here. Hope you like your new job."

From Grand Pré, N.S.: "How would you like to live in a place like this? Don't you think there is some class to it? B. H."

From Southampton, Ont., to Owen Sound: "Do you like Owen Sound? We roast one day and freeze the next as usual. Do you attend League? Do you ever think of coming back to Southampton?"

"League" is often mentioned and we are told it meant the Epworth League which was basically a young people's organization of Methodist affiliation, and the sponsor of such social events as readings, concerts, sing-songs, and picnics.

The Edwardians thought fondly of home and liked to return often: "Dear Father and Mother—How are the roads down that way now? If it is fine next Saturday, I am coming down if the old boat will carry me that far."

On balance the messages reflect happy home lives: "I suppose Stan is home by this time and you have a game of checkers. Pa had a birthday today—71 and he looks fine and never was better for years. Millie."

Longing for their own small town keeps tugging at them: "I find out that there are worse places than Weston." And this card to Bloomfield, N.S.: "It is nice in Toronto but oh! how I like it down at your place." Again the refrain: "Bertha likes Toronto all right but not as nice as Orillia. I don't like it as much as Orillia either."

Western towns experienced phenomenal growth during these years. A special census was taken of the North West provinces in 1906, and increases in population, especially in Saskatchewan and Alberta, are startling. Davidson, Saskatchewan, didn't exist in 1901 but had 520 people in 1906; Pense had 15 inhabitants in 1901 and 185 in 1906. High River, Alberta, had 153 in 1901; it boasted 1,018 in 1906. Nanton was prairie in 1901 but 382 lived there in 1906. Carpenters must have had a field-day in the West of those days, though many homes, naturally, were built by their owners.

Almost everyone who went West in those days liked it. Here is a 1911 message from Daysland, Alta.: "This is just a view of one of the many towns in the West. This certainly is a great country."

From Brandon, Man., to Toronto, Ont., 1911: "I don't

know how the drug business is, this is the country to come to for everything or at least, anything. I am going to stay at this job until next summer. This is a peach of a town. I am going to stick around."

Here is a qualified approval from Carson, Sask.: "I like the West much better than the East though I formerly lived in the East myself near Peterborough, Ontario. I think there are much better opportunities here and I also like the climate better as it is much drier and healthier, though at present it is not very nice being cold and very windy, lots of dust."

But not all were euphoric. Here's a toughie from Cochrane, Alta., to Ormstown, Que.: "Dear Dad—This is Cochrane as you can see, but if you could only smell the dirt! For the last hour I have held my handkerchief to my nose. It has Edmonton beaten a mile for dust. Love, Eunice."

And this cryptic note: North Battleford, Sask., February 3, 1908: "Am pretty well fed up on the Northwest. . . ."

In the pages following we will ramble across Canada from one coast to another looking at towns and villages as they were in Edwardian times.

Cupids—Guy's first Settlement.

John Guy, a Bristol merchant, was appointed first Governor of Newfoundland in 1612.

Ship Cove, Burine, Nfld.

Old Church at Placentia.

Harbour Grace, Nfld., to Whitbourne, June 22, 1908: "Dear Lizzie— Sending Tea by Express, Flour & Butter as freight. . . . Love to All. T. L. J."

Fogo district welcomes President Coaker
A chat with the President on board the Motor boat F. P. U.

"Fogo district welcomes President Coaker", founder of the Newfoundland Fisherman's Protective Union. William F. Coaker established the first local of the union in 1908.

PIONEER FAMILY, FIVE GENERATIONS TIDNISH, P.E.I.

"Tidnish" is a printer's error; the family resided at Tignish, P.E.I.

Bear River, N.S.: "Dear Agnes—Can't you do anything with that sister of yours to make her stop flirting with my young man? I am feeling miserable over it you know. . . . Gertrude."

The Old Red Bridge, Bridgetown, N.S., "was torn down this fall for a new iron one. You just see it a little way right from our station when you come to Bridgetown. Wishing you all a Merry Xmas, E. A. R."

Yarmouth, N.S., to Havelock, Digby County: "My dear Frank — I am so lonesome. I was looking for a letter from you today but I didn't get any and I was so disappointed. I would love to see you tonight. . . . Maud."

Campobello, N.B.

St. Stephen, N.B., to Melrose, Mass., August 2, 1914: "I thought I would write you from Canada. It is so different here. You must drive on the left side of the road and there is a one-hour difference in time owing to the time belt."

MR MC KAW RESIDENCE COTEAU LANDING

Coteau Landing, Que.

The left border of the card reads: "See you tonight. We will have to be satisfied with the pleasant thoughts of last night."

"Je pense *toujours* à toi et à mes chères petites filles. . . . Louis."

Yonge Street, Aurora, Ont.

Berlin's name was changed to Kitchener in 1916.

The aftermath of a gas explosion in the business section of Brantford, Ont., September 11, 1908. Five buildings were destroyed and two lives lost.

"This is Burgoyne store and the Tara stage calling to get the Mail Bag. Also Mr. Cameron, the store keeper."

Coppercliff, Ont., February 1, 1909: "x marks the Methodist Church; v marks the Presbyterian Church. Hurry up and write to—J. C."

A stark reminder of the Edwardian poor.

Canal Street, Dunnville, Ont., during the flood of 1913.

Elora, Ont., to Guelph, May 2, 1910: "Hello Lizzie — This is a photo of the main street taken after the ice storm we had during the winter. Doesn't it look terrible. . . . Maggie."

Section of Main Street looking West. Galt, Canada.

"I am still looking for a nice girl to do my cooking and keep me company in the evenings, and have no luck in Galt."

Manitowaning is on Manitoulin Island.

"This is a snapshot of the awful collapse of a couple of our buildings in London. . . . I knew nearly all who lost their lives there."

An uncommon card entitled "The Gypsies". Mattawa is in the Ottawa Valley lumbering country.

Note the sign on the tree at left: "Souvenir Postcards—Best in Town."

A competitor on Sydney Street boasts: "We lead in Souvenir Post Cards."

Iroquois was one of the villages along the St. Lawrence flooded by the seaway.

Windsor Mills, Que., to Sherbrooke, April 18, 1910: "Dearest Lina—I went yesterday to the play 'The Schoolmistress'; it was just splendid. I saw Mr. C. there but he would not look where I was at all. . . . Lots of Love, Pauline."

The Brant Hotel or Inn was popular with Hamilton and area residents.

This card, postmarked August 1911, shows the new Hotel Quinte. The old hotel burned to the ground in January 1906.

ST. GEORGE'S CHURCH AND FOOT
BRIDGE, GUELPH, ONT.
643
CANADA
Dear Ethel
Am with Mrs Park
going to Caladonia
tomorrow.
Will not be
home this
week. Did Edya
come out. Poor
hammock worse
of wear. Mrs Daves
serious, Maggie in
Jarvis. all is well
Fred W not at home
Having a quiet pleasant
time. Love to Lib &
all. Lovingly yours
THE EMPIRE UPON WHICH
THE SUN NEVER SETS.
NORTH MAIN STREET,
HAGERSVILLE, ONT.
COPYRIGHTED 1904 BY ATKINSON BROS.

Princess Street, Kingston, Ont., Canada
SUTHERLAND
101675

DRUGGIST
Talbot Street East, Leamington, Ont.

MAIN STREET, NEWMARKET, ONT.
King Street, Midland, Canada
View in Queen's Park, London, Canada.
MARTHA WAGENFUHRER.
MAID OF NIAGARA FALLS RAPIDS.
Shot the Whirlpool Rapids on Sept. 6, 1901. Barrel on Exhibition at Niagara Falls Museum.

Hiram T. Bush was mayor and chief magistrate of Port Hope from 1913 to 1915.

The Aberdeen Bridge opened in 1894. It was a swing bridge, allowing sailing vessels to pass through.

The first McLaughlin car, a Model F, was built in December 1907, and sold at $1,400, top or windshield extra.

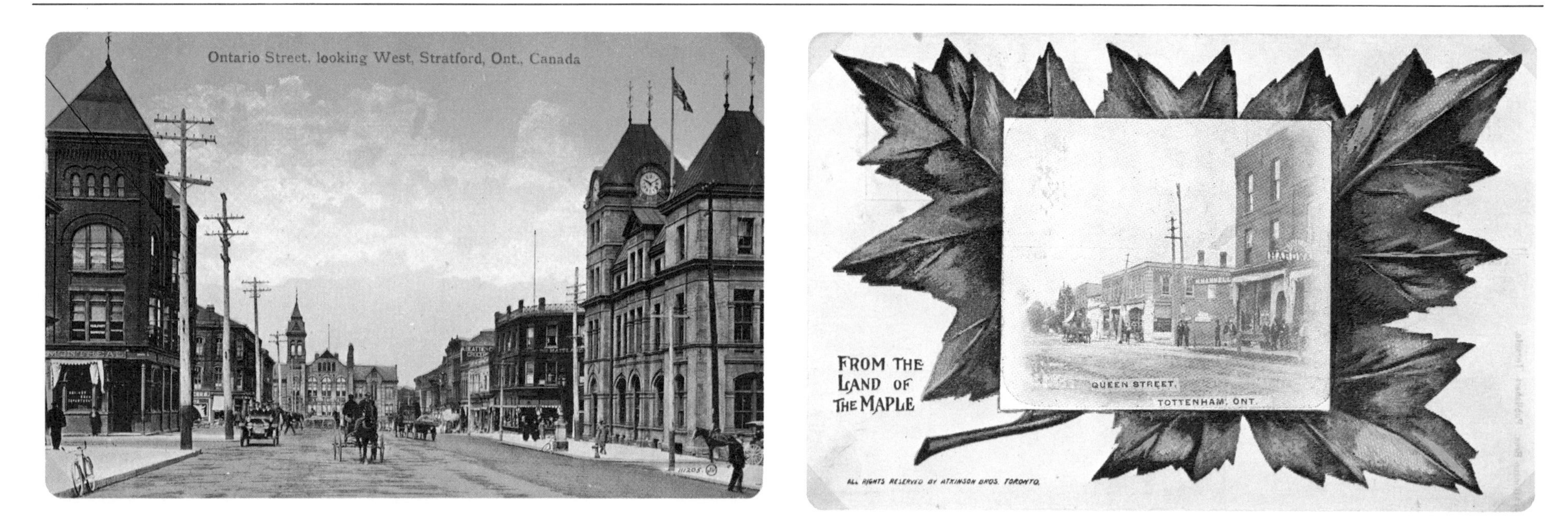
Ontario Street, looking West, Stratford, Ont., Canada
FROM THE LAND OF THE MAPLE
QUEEN STREET.
TOTTENHAM, ONT.
ALL RIGHTS RESERVED BY ATKINSON BROS. TORONTO.

Main Street, Unionville, Ont., Canada

Residential Street, Brandon,

Traffic Bridge over Saskatchewan River, Medicine Hat, Alta, Canada

Wetaskiwin on a busy day. Wetaskiwin, Alta.

A Stroll to Visit the Coal Mines — Nanaimo, B. C.

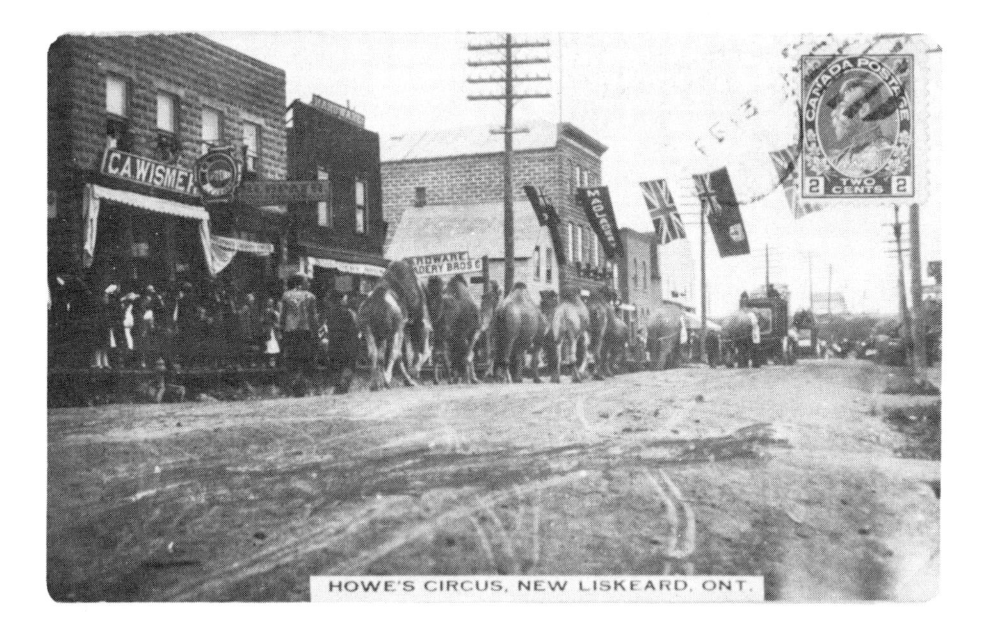

"This is the hotel where we are stopping. I am tired, the girl is tired, and so is the horse. . . ."

Parry Sound, Ont., to London, March 20, 1909: "Parry Sound on a busy day. You will notice the B. of Toronto in the foreground. I'm still waiting, Lily. Dave."

The banner proclaims the Peterborough Industrial Exhibition and prizes of $3,000 in cash.

OLD CREDIT RIVER BRIDGE
HAMILTON HIGHWAY
PT CREDIT ONT.
PRICEVILLE.
ONT.
Market and Town Hall, Prescott., Ont., Can.
The Wire Bridge, Renfrew, Ont.

Covered bridge, Trenton, Ont. As far as is known, this was one of only seven covered bridges in the province. It had six spans and one lifted to allow sailboats to pass underneath.

Wallaceburg, Ont., to Port Dover, May 1910: "Dear Lilly — If I could only stop or flag this fellow in the air ship I might run over to Port Dover. . . . Ever, Milt."

Elevators at Pierson, Man.

"This is the wonderful town of Strathclair. Hotel is right in the centre."

Westerners took quickly to the automobile, and new owners were happy to line up for the photographer.

Mrs. M. Sabin drove a bull and cart once a week from the Goose Lake country to Hanley to pick up the local mail.

A horse-drawn stage leaves the Imperial Hotel at Indian Head, Sask.

Pense, Sask., twenty miles west of Regina, was an important equipment depot during the construction of the CPR.

Business was obviously booming for this smiling North Battleford real estate broker.

Main Street, Swift Current, Sask.

Watrous, Sask., to Fort William, Ont.: "Hello, Minnie. See where we are now. . . . This is a swell little town, going to have a dip in the lake this afternoon. Maud."

"Yorkton, N.W.T." The North West Territories became the provinces of Alberta and Saskatchewan in 1905.

1st Avenue, Brooks, Alta.

Street View, High River, Alta.

ALBERTA HOTEL, MEDICINE HAT, ALBERTA, CANADA.

Now a ghost town, Steveville, in east central Alberta, was once noted for its annual July 1 ball tournament, which drew crowds from miles around.

"I move into my shack tonight. There is a stable for my cayuse too. I preached once yesterday but will have more stations by next Sunday since I have a pony and can get around more."

Strathcona, Alta., March 8, 1911: "This is the car we take every time we go to Edmonton. . . . " Strathcona amalgamated with Edmonton in 1912.

Originally called Union, the town name was changed to Cumberland by coal magnate James Dunsmuir in 1891. Many of his miners had emigrated from Cumberland, England.

"Hello, Sweet—I thought Smithers was bad enough but this is worse, they don't even have the board sidewalks here and no show or a darn thing, not even a pool table. . . ."

Powell River, B.C.: "All houses painted different colours, built of wood, looks like exhibition grounds, electric lights throughout—free!"

Phoenix, now a ghost town, once boasted twenty-eight saloons, five dance halls, and a boarding house where 400 miners fought over a single girl.

Powell River, B.C.: "Many are roughly dressed, as they have just a coat over sports clothes, including me. . . ."

Prince Rupert, B.C., to Bournemouth, England, July 1909: "Dear Hilda and all—This is just a card to show the excitement that exists over real estate here. For four days people crowded outside this office from 7 A.M. to 8 P.M. . . . I'm sending on a paper showing prices paid. Much love, B."

Stewart, B.C., to Goderich, Ont., July 4, 1910: "Dear Mother—I am a 3rd partner in this business doing $500.00 to $1,000.00 a day, right in the centre of a rich mining camp. . . . Frank."

Fairs & Exhibitions

EVERYONE LOOKED FORWARD to the fall fair and those who had moved to towns or cities were always eager to get home to take in the local festivities. The fairs served a very important social purpose—when time or distance did not allow for easy visiting, one could meet friends from all over the township or county at the fairgrounds. Almost as soon as the first settlers harvested their crops in Ontario, there were agricultural societies and competitive exhibitions. The Maritimes also got off to an early start; Nova Scotia was the first to stage an agricultural fair. The Stanley Fair, outside Fredericton, has a long and famous history.

Around 1900 in Ontario there was much grumbling about fairs and complaints of poor judging, disdain for professional exhibitors, and alarms raised about the quality of entertainment. In 1902 a Whitby reporter commented, "The horse race and the fakir should not be among the attractive features. . . . There is something very fascinating and exciting about a horse race but there is so much gambling and jockeyism associated with it, that it has been in late years simply a farce."

There were dozens of fairs and exhibitions in Western Canada before 1890. The first fair in the West was held at Victoria in 1861, but fairs and exhibitions soon became popular in Brandon, Regina, Saskatoon, Calgary, Edmonton, and Vancouver. The fullest account of a good fair comes from Stonewall, Man., in a message to Elmwood, Ont., October 5, 1913: "I was at the show here and everything was something extra, potatoes and all the vegetables were nice and large and also the fancy work was beautiful and the work done by school scholars was wonderful too."

"Dear Lizzie—We are still on the gad & having a high time. Not a man yet but we are thinking of going back to the exhibition after dinner to look for them. Mollie."

Richmond Hill, Ont.

New Westminster, B.C., to Iowa, December 28, 1911: "Billie — I went to Vancouver today to look for a man and they all looked alike except the handsome Hindus, but they won't look at a pretty young thing like me. . . ."

"We arrived home safe but it was dreadful dark. . . . We did not get to Onondaga Fair, may see you at Caledonia yet. From Annie."

Machinery Exhibit, Brandon, Man.

I Love a Parade

THAT FAMILIAR TITLE could well be a theme song for the Edwardians. They would crowd the streets or perch themselves dangerously on balconies to watch and cheer the bands and marchers. There were inaugural processions for towns and cities, Dominion Day parades, Labour Day assemblies, and Old Boy reunions. The Glorious Twelfth was for many the greatest event of all. The Orangemen were in their glory in those days: Kincardine, Ont., July 12, 1911: "Am here today with the band and Orangemen. Big crowd of people here and nice town."

The power and sway of the Orange Order in Canada baffled Englishmen visiting the country. In 1903, A. G. Bradley wrote: "It is true you will still find Orangemen in Canada who believe themselves to be the sole bulwark against the enslavement of the world by the Pope and his minions, and decent farmers or mere working men will entertain you with such convictions on this subject as have not been heard in England for eighty years."

Parades, like fall fairs, were events that were eagerly looked forward to and long discussed in careful and often critical detail afterwards.

The Glorious Twelfth and a salute to "King Billy".

Twelfth of July parade at Alliston, Ont., in 1909.

Clinton, Ont., June 9, 1909: "Hello, Grace—This picture was when Sir Wilfrid Laurier was here. See if you can find him on the platform. . . ."

The citizenry of Orangeville, Ont., celebrate a major victory of the Boer War, the relief of Ladysmith on February 28, 1900. The war ended in 1902.

Preston, Ont., was well-known to Canadians and Americans for its mineral springs.

Decoration Day services were held in the spring; traditionally, it was a day when people visited cemeteries to tidy family plots and plant flowers.

European homesteaders in the West were sometimes called "foreign settlers". Premier R. P. Roblin of Manitoba, in a famous speech delivered at Picton, Ont., in June 1907, declared it was only a matter of time before these people "could if they chose take all matter of government absolutely into their own hands."

Labour Day at Fort William, Ont., 1906. A comment on the reverse side reads: "I think they have invested in a box of bow ties."

A delivery of Massey Harris equipment to Rodney, Ont., in 1913 creates an instant parade.

Renfrew, Ont., Golden Jubilee, 1908.

This rare card shows an extraordinary event: a demonstration by the Sinn Fein, the Irish nationalist group, in Saskatoon on Labour Day, 1912, during a visit of the Governor General, the Duke of Connaught.

Empire Day, May 24, at Prince Albert, Sask.

Alberta became a province on September 1, 1905, and Edmonton celebrated. Residents were given a whole week of free power — all the electricity they could use.

The Duke and Duchess of Connaught toured Canada in 1912 and Vancouver's CPR station was decked in splendour to greet the Governor General's party.

School Days

Among the most charming of all Edwardian postcards are those of school children clustered outside the school house. Teachers were caricatured as prim creatures, but in fact they were usually a very lively lot who worked hard and were very popular.

This message, sent from Stratford, Ont., to Berlin, November 25, 1911, attests to the long hours: "Spent all of tonight and last night on plan for lesson for Tuesday. Wish the lessons were over. Have a bad attack of indigestion—the result of late breakfasts I think. I generally get up at 6:00 and often don't have breakfast till about 8:30. Love to Lizzy, Maud."

Yet this message from Boissevain, Man., to Watrous, Sask., is characteristic: September 12, 1909: "I am busily engaged teaching Grades 3 and 4 here. They have 2 fine schools here and employ 7 teachers. My work is very easy and my room is newly equipped. It is the prettiest school room I ever saw; it surpasses any I saw in Winnipeg."

There are frequent references to the size of their classes: Fort William, Ont., to Guelph, October 19, 1910: "Fine school these days. 48 little people on the roll, 47 there today." And of course school attendance would drop when there was farm work to keep the youngsters home. To Tarton, Ont., from Leadbury, September 30, 1912: "I am right at home all the time as I am teaching my home school. I have about 40 on roll but 26 is all I have had yet. People are working at harvest."

And when their teaching days were over, there was often regret: "I get lonesome for my pupils and the dry air of the prairies."

This intriguing card is from Lanark, Ont., to Peterborough, May 18, 1907: "Had a letter from M. in Manitoba. They want me to take the Treherne School, $650.00 and board. J. G. and his 2 brother-in-laws are trustees so I won't have no trouble in getting it, but I am so afraid of the consequences. Pretty maiden with a book, man rides past—makes a mash. I got a P. card of twins fighting for a bottle and under was written, is marriage a failure? You have nothing to do so write soon. M."

We can only speculate on the outcome.

Earl Grey School—but the locale is unknown. Many schools were named for Earl Grey, Governor General of Canada from 1904 to 1911.

PRIVATE POST CARD
Address to be written on this side
Stamp.

Miss E. J. Neibel
School Teacher and
Kid Puncher.

A school in Grand Falls, Nfld., "where Bertha works".

ONTARIO AGRICULTURAL COLLEGE.
Guelph, Ont. July 18th, '05.

Dear Sir,-

Farmers are entitled to as good an education as anybody. We have had good boys from your County before, and we are prepared to admit on Sept. the 15th other students from about your home. I shall esteem it a favor if you will be so kind as to send me on the attached card the names and addresses of a few young men between the ages of 17 and 25 in your district, who would likely be interested in literature regarding the course of instruction in our College.

Very truly yours,
G. C. Creelman.

The public school at Cochrane in northern Ontario.

The Ontario government bought a farm on the outskirts of Guelph in 1873, which was later to become the Ontario Agricultural College.

On November 20, 1905, during afternoon recess, fire broke out in the furnace room, and this 1889 school burned to the ground.

"This is part of my school last year at Foxwarren, Manitoba, taken on the day of the school picnic, June 3, 1911. Cameron."

A class at Indian Head, Sask.

Quinton, Sask., 1912: "This is our class at school. Doris Kitchen is the first by the door, I am the fourth on the same row."

"Dear Etta & Beatrice—I received the results yesterday from Mr. Welsh & wish to congratulate you both. We shall get the Algebra fixed up next year."

Fire!

FIRE SPELLED CATASTROPHE for small towns and villages. A community might be devastated not once, but two or three times over a period of years. Little could be done to save wooden buildings, and fires often started on a windy day when a spark from a foundry, for instance, would set a building ablaze.

The cities were just as much prey to fire, as witness the terrible Toronto fire of 1904. Many a conflagration originated with overheated stoves and furnaces, often in the dead of winter when the temperature was 20 degrees below. One Montreal card, dated December 12, 1906, shows a building festooned with enormous icicles. The message reads: "After one of our little fires of the other day." The card shows a seven-storey building completely razed. On the front of the ruin is a sign saying "the greatest fire sale that ever took place in Canada." Business was as enterprising then as now.

Fire departments of the Edwardian era often depended on jet-black Percheron horses, the best money could buy, to pull the fire wagons. The horses stood loose in box stalls and when the alarm sounded the stalls were opened and the horses were hurried into position. Complete sets of harness dropped from the ceiling to the horses' backs, the heavy collars were coupled, snapped shut, straps buckled, and away they went at a gallop. The whole process took less than a minute.

Think of the excitement generated by the sight of those huge black Percherons tearing out of the firehall with the cumbersome equipment rocking behind them!

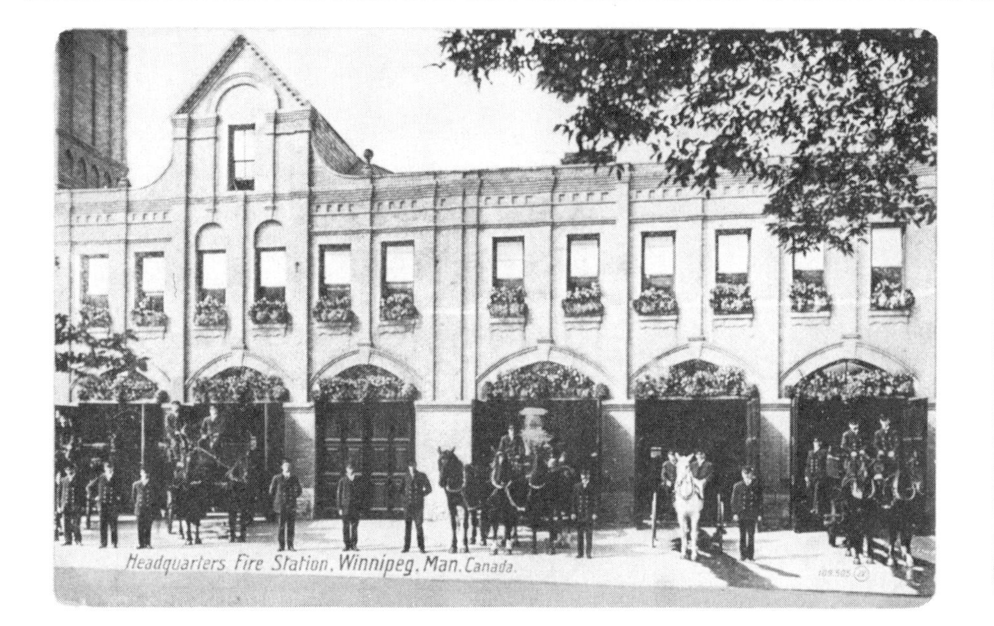
Headquarters Fire Station, Winnipeg, Man. Canada.

Lombard St. Fire Hall, Toronto.

Fire Hall, Vancouver. B.C.

Fire Hall, Moose Jaw, Canada

From Original Photograph by Lewis Rice. Rights Reserved.

Eighty-six buildings were destroyed in this major Toronto fire in the downtown area; five thousand people were temporarily out of work, but miraculously, no lives were lost.

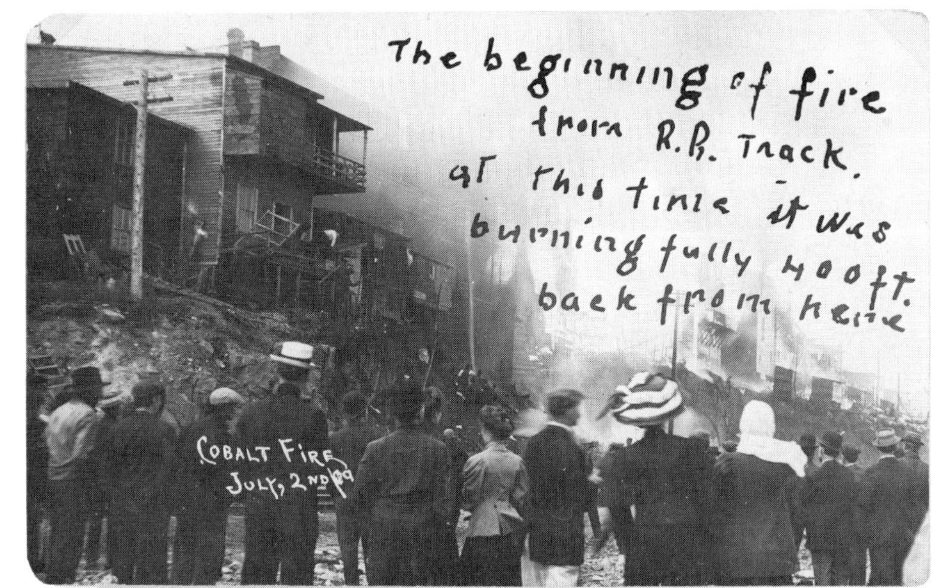

An unknown man and a young girl were the victims of this July 2, 1909, fire in Cobalt, Ont. It began in a Chinese restaurant and swept north destroying 200 homes and stores.

The July 1911 fire in South Porcupine, Ont., took 73 lives, covered 864 square miles, and destroyed gold-mine property worth $3,000,000.

Halifax, N.S., January 22, 1912: "Dear Eveline—This shows you the effects of a big fire here in mid-winter with the temperature below zero. The loss was somewhere near $500,000."

Indians & Esquimaux

INDIAN CARDS FROM THE EDWARDIAN ERA are bright and colourful, and collectors hunt them down relentlessly. There are cards depicting various tribes, from Micmacs in the Maritimes to Songhees on the west coast. Seldom do messages refer to the Indians pictured on the card. Usually, as on a lovely card of a papoose in the Georgian Bay area, there is a totally unrelated message: "Dear Sid—I am sending you my picture, thanks for the rings, our cats are well."

Occasionally, the messages do refer directly to the scene on the card. There is one sent from Victoria, B.C., to Kent, England, showing an Indian dugout canoe with eight occupants. The 1906 message reads: "Many thanks for pretty post card. This canoe is very natural and is like the Indians used to go to war in."

In Edwardian times, people exhibited an unconscious bigotry. The white man was better than anyone else; it was that simple. The result is messages such as: "I am still here, expect to quit when my month is in as they have got squaws and Chinese coming here."

Not everyone, however, thought that way. There is a straightforward picture of a Temagami Indian guide and his family in this section. The message reads: "I have not seen the Indians as rough as this, they are a smart lot of people that I have seen, the girls are neat."

There are very few early "Esquimaux" cards to be found, and those that do show up are of Labrador Inuit. The very first cards in our collection were of Barren Land Inuit but these were cards of a slightly later date than the Edwardian period. Nevertheless, we prize them highly; they got us started on the long trek in search of Edwardian cards.

Showman Buffalo Bill and part of his entourage at Fort Garry, Winnipeg.

Algonquin Indian Guide and Family, Temagami District, Ontario

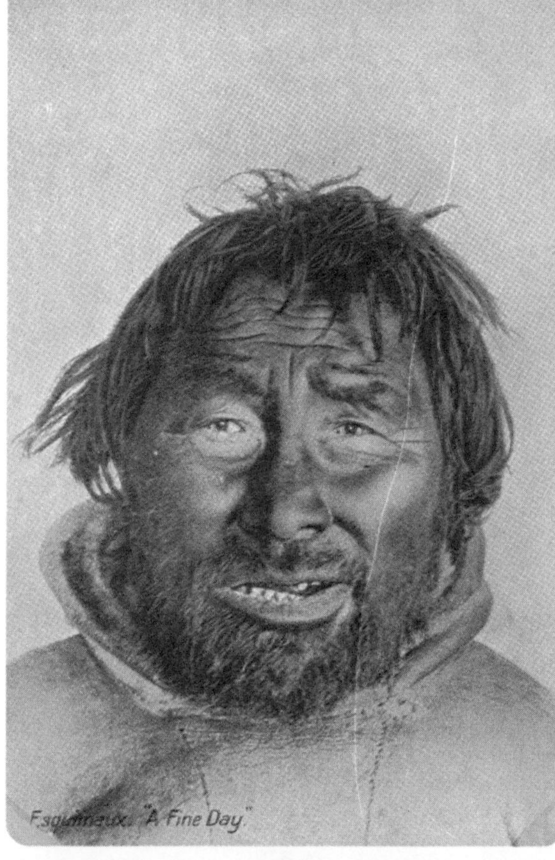
Esquimaux. "A Fine Day"

Hudson's Bay Esquimaux.

Esquimaux in Traders Hut.

"The city is full of real western farmers, cowboys, and Indians, with all their paint and buckskins, here for the Exhibition. Love from Papa."

"Say, boy, have you got your potatoes and turnips up? Have you got your apples pulled? If not you had better get a move on. . . ."

Harvesting, near Edmonton, Alta., Canada

In the Wheat Fields of Saskatchewan
CANADA'S
GOLDEN WEST

Schooner " James William " First steel sailing vessel built in Nova Scotia.

MARKET SLIP, ST. JOHN, N.B.

PRINCESS VICTORIA

When the Canadian navy was formed in 1910, the British navy withdrew completely from the dockyards at Halifax and Esquimalt. This card is dated 1907.

There's bustle and excitement at the Gravenhurst, Ont., wharf as the Grand Trunk unloads passengers eager to get to cottages and resorts.

Canadians crowded the observation cars, enduring smoke and cinders.

Station on White Pass and Yukon Route at Summit of White Pass. International Boundary between Alaska and Canada

C.P.R. Station, Galt, Ont., Canada

"Indian Dance, Batoche" (Sask.).

"Crees on the way to see the Sioux play football."

Photo taken at Medicine Hat, Alta.

The Tahltan Indians are a tribe of the Nahanni in B.C.

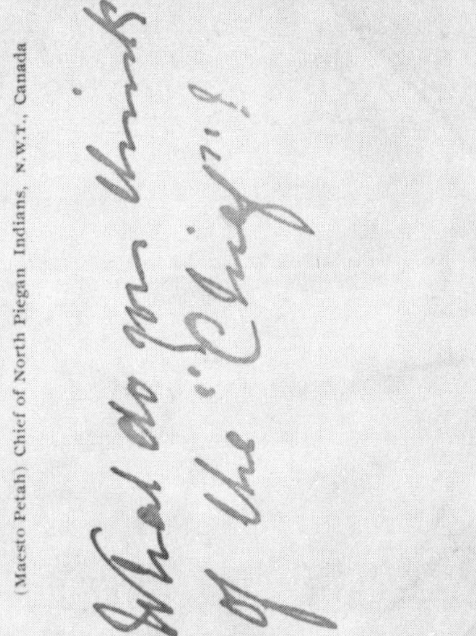

TOTEM POLES SKIDEGATE B. C.

Kyaking at Turnavick, Labrador.

A Little Native of Labrador.

Breaking the Sod

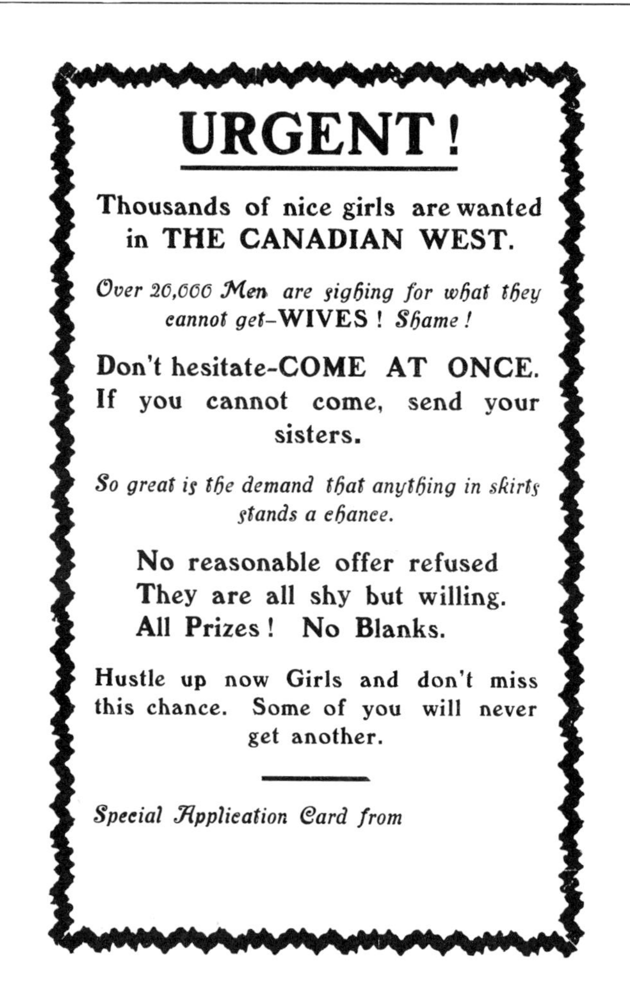
URGENT!

Thousands of nice girls are wanted in THE CANADIAN WEST.

Over 20,000 Men are sighing for what they cannot get–WIVES! *Shame!*

Don't hesitate–COME AT ONCE. If you cannot come, send your sisters.

So great is the demand that anything in skirts stands a chance.

No reasonable offer refused
They are all shy but willing.
All Prizes! No Blanks.

Hustle up now Girls and don't miss this chance. Some of you will never get another.

Special Application Card from

HOMESTEADING SURELY QUALIFIES as the definitive Canadian experience of the Edwardian years. The eager prospects, the loneliness and unending struggle, the failures and successes — all are evident in the messages on the postals sent home. From Rosthern, Sask., to Toronto, Ont., September 23, 1909: "I've never been so busy in all my life. I guess this is the first time I've done real work. And it 'hoits my noives'. I'm getting quite chesty however, over my success."

From Alameda, Sask., 1909: "Dear Sister—Made an offer for a half-section. Waiting for an answer probably Friday or Saturday. Half of Ontario is up here and lots of Americans."

Here is a card sent to Minnesota from the Canadian West: "Say, young fellow, better come where they do things and get a fresh hold and grow up with the country and not be stubbing around among the rocks and stones. George."

And here is a great message to the folks back home in Springville, Ont., from Ernfold, Sask.: "Hello Sid—It's great sport homesteading. We have got a shack up to keep out the rain till we get our house up. It is 10 x 12. We have to move everything out of it when we want to get in and everything in when we go away."

Unpredictable weather and freak accidents were constant preoccupations. Gull Lake, Sask., to Wiarton, Ont., March 17, 1910: "I am homesteading now this winter and it is very cold, sometimes about 48 below. Write soon. Albert."

From Wallacetown, Ont., to Leamington: "Just got word from Jack, he is in the hospital in Moose Jaw. Broke his leg last Thursday, did not get it set until the next day at noon, they were 30 miles out to homestead with loads. E. D."

Even in matters romantic it was nothing ventured, nothing gained. This card is to Jessie in St. Catharines, Ont., from Cayley, Alta.: "My dear Jessie—I am a lonesome bachelor living on the Prairies. Have to bake my own bread and sew on my buttons and darn socks. If you think you would like living in the West let me know and there may be something doing. P.S. Please send your picture. Yours to a cinder, Firman C."

Bernard, Sask.: "Suppose the harvest is in full swing down there. I was going to try to get down for the harvest but I was too busy. Eby has new binder. He says the next thing he gets is a wife. The same here, ha, ha! Goodbye. Sid."

"In front of Dominion Lands Office, Sept. 1st, '08, Estevan, Sask."

Oxen sold at half the price of horses, but they travelled at half the speed.

"Dear Frank—Your card received. So you are thinking of going homesteading, that will be quite a change from the office. . . ."

The whole family poses for a photograph, and mother wears her best hat to impress the relatives back East.

Blocks of sod cut from the virgin prairie were laid on top of one another to form walls; a structure of poles supported the roof.

"Dear Neice—This is a photo of a neighbour (John Wilson). It explains itself."

Delisle, Sask., September 7, 1906: "Dear Brother—This is our new barn on homestead. It will hold 8 head of horses, we have 6. . . . I expected to see you out on the harvest excursion, you are missing the treat of your life. J. Loucks."

Delisle, Sask., April 26, 1911: "Hello, how are you all getting along. . . . We started to seed on the 17 and today we have over 200 acres in. That is the way we go out west. . . . J. Loucks."

A Special Breed

A MOST LUCID AND ENTERTAINING ACCOUNT of the Edwardian rancher is given in *Canada as it Is*, by John Foster Frazer, published in 1905. He says,

As you sit on the stoop of the little hotel at Macleod, Alberta, you talk and smoke with ranchers—old timers many of them. They are lithe and scraggy-framed, big-fisted, and shamble-gaited; their cheeks have been yellowed and wrinkled with sun and snow glare; heavy wrinkles on either side of the eyes. They are unshaven and uncombed; their clothes are baggy and unfitting, and their hats are ready for the scare-crow. They sit loungingly cross-legged, talk in a drone but confidentially, smoke incessantly, and expectorate unceasingly. You pick out a man you don't think worth 10¢. He is really worth $50,000, not in hard cash, but in cattle.

"No, sir; ranching ain't what it was," says he. "In the old days we squatted on the foothills where there was good feed and water. We haven't got the snows they have back in the middle west. The cattle just grew into money. But now, with the in-rush of settlers getting homesteads, and buying land from the government, we ranchers are being pushed back into the hills."

Ranchers wanted an open range. They looked down on anyone who got off a horse except to eat and sleep, and they detested settlers. There were some powder-keg situations between ranchers and homesteaders; the range was set afire at times by settlers and ranchers would bar homesteaders from the waterholes, but incidents of gun play were exceedingly rare.

The romance of ranching is epitomized in the popular mind by the stampede, and among the greatest stampede pictures ever taken were those of Doc Marcell. Marcell left his Portland, Oregon, photographic studio to come to Calgary in 1912. Some of his tremendous action shots are included in this section as are his photographs of the Winnipeg Stampede of 1913. An interesting feature of these early stampedes is the participation of women. They came out of the shoots riding and roping with the best of them, displaying the courage and stamina that made them a breed unto themselves.

Financially successful easterners, senators, and businessmen bought huge spreads in the West. This message is obviously written by a woman accustomed to another social life: Brant, Alta., September 1911: "Dear Isabel—Doesn't it seem a long time since the June ball. I've been to several western dances and such a contrast. I like them all the same. Do write. N. R. W."

Here is a message from a woman writing to a friend in the area; by the sound of it she too was a relative newcomer to ranching: Long View, Alta., September 7, 1913: "Hello Girly—Here I am, fine and dandy. Having a fine change. Len is here and we are holding down the ranch. Have been driving a lot and was for a long ride on horseback Sunday night. Of course I am feeling the effects now."

The famous Bar-U Ranch was located near High River, Alta.

A
HARD FALL
WINNIPEG STAMPEDE 1913.
PHOTO No 4. © CAN. BY MARCELL OF CALGARY
HASEL WALKER THROWN BY "BUTTONS". "BUT SHE RODE HIM JUST THE SAME."
"THE STAMPEDE" CALGARY ALTA 1912. OFFICIAL PHOTO No 54.
MARCELL
HORSE CONTEST
MOOSE JAW STAMPEDE 1916
COPYRIGHT APPLIED FOR
LUCILLE MULHALL
CHAMPION LADY STEER ROPER
OF THE WORLD.
WINNIPEG STAMPEDE 1913.
TIME - 33 1/5th SEC.
PHOTO 42. © CAN-U.S.A
MARCELL OF CALGARY

Remembering the Farm

By JUNE 1, 1911, there were in round figures 715,000 farms in Canada and almost 4,000,000 people living on them, out of a total population of just over 7,000,000. Not surprisingly, then, many postcard messages reported daily happenings on the farm. Let us start with this fine cheerful one from Prince Edward Island: "The farm is the place to rest. All I can hear at the present is the hum of the hay cutters."

Many of the messages are of the "could you give us a hand" variety. From Humberstone, Ont., to Port Colborne, May 10: "Dear Father—Could you come up Friday morning and help Arthur fix the pig-pens if it suits you. Arthur cannot work on the land for a few days. Please bring that bushel of New Yorker potatoes along for seed. Your daughter. Mary."

Everybody on the farm was busy and, usually, cheerful. From Conestogo, Ont., to Berlin, October 2, 1909: "Dear Mabel—I am kept quite busy as I still run a boarding house. We are going to cut corn next week and I will have 14 men to cook for. I made some short cakes yesterday. They were very good too. . . . Why don't you take a walk up some day when you have lots of time. I'll keep you over night just the same as any other tramp. Ha. Ha. Laura."

From Waterville, N.S., to Halifax, December 8, 1912: "We are going to dress the hens tomorrow. I just dread the dirty job. Will be glad when it is done. Father is to butcher the pigs Tuesday, we will be glad to get some lard. Just two weeks and two days before Christmas. We will have lots of butter by that time. Aggie."

When a farmer was laid low by illness, the women took over. From Frankford, Ont., to Consecon, August 1: "We are going as hard as ever at our berries and hay. We pick as high as 225 quarts. We had 4 men and 2 teams drawing hay today. But have half a day yet to draw. Us girls have been horse raking and mowing away hay and so has ma. Pa is getting worse all the time. Can't scarcely talk or eat. He is very poor, weighs 101 pounds."

Occasionally there is talk of quilting bees: November 9, 1911: "Dear Cora—We won't be down this week, we are having our bee today. I have to bake bread tomorrow and kill ducks to take to town on Saturday. Betty."

In August, the harvesters headed West where there was work for every man. Walpole, Sask., to Stouffville, Ont., September 10, 1908: "Was to Walpole today. I go with a threshing outfit Monday and will be with it for about 30 days or so. Albert."

Harvesting was a harried time for all: "People teaming their grain in now, is all that is going on now. Some days there are 150 locals in, so many has to stay over night with their oxen." Similarly, this message from Greenshields, Alta., to Todmorden, Ont., October 4: "The farmers are busy loading cars at the station with wheat and oats, they are going from 6 in the morning till 12 at night."

Many are the messages like this one from Ethel in Ninga, Man.: "I hope your cows go dry for a few days or a week, so you can come down and see me after the busy time is over."

Finally the long winter would arrive and, after an eternity, spring would return to the farm. From Hamiota, Man.: "How do you like spring, I just revel in the muck and slush something like 'the widder's pig'."

"Everything all to the merry here. Finished threshing yesterday, will start in plowing with the engine Monday."

"Got our potatoes in and finished threshing this week, going to Henry's to help fill silo. . . . Pa said he would get me a buggy next spring."

44 — Stacking at Myrtle (Man:)
L. J. De Nobele Import, Winnipeg

N. Weters Threshing Outfit 1908.

Steam Plowing, Francis, Sask.

An odd team, Netherhill, Sask.
COPYRIGHTED in Canada

Off to the Grain Fields, Western Canada

Typical Canadian North West Scene Saving Time on the Farm.

"Mr. V. with whom we are staying has a 1,200 acre farm 3 miles from town. The finest wheat and oats I ever saw. If frosts stay off for three weeks he will have at least 15,000 bushels of grain."

To The Elevators, Western Canada

Grain elevators were erected on the prairies about 1880. By 1916-17 country elevators in the three prairie provinces numbered 3,287.

To Market, To Market

POSTCARDS OF EARLY MARKETS are beautiful specimens of the art of hand colouring. The detail is precise, with buggies, wagons, crowds of people, all very distinct. You not only see the market site, but the vivid realism is such that you can easily imagine the sustained buzz of conversation and the constant rush of traffic.

Scenes of western markets are scarce, though they certainly existed. In other cases, however, there are as many as six different views of certain markets—Hamilton, for instance.

Market halls, many of which were magnificent buildings, have been altered in recent years without any regard for the aesthetic quality of the building, or they simply have been torn down and done away with. One of the great attractions of a large collection of Edwardian postcards is that it is possible to see in detail long-vanished buildings and even whole city blocks, and to appreciate the immense variety of Edwardian architecture.

Here is a pleasantly newsy message on the back of a view of the market square at Chatham, Ontario. The month was September, the year 1910, and the card was sent from Chatham to Owen Sound:

Dear Mother—This is Labour Day and my afternoon to work. We saw a fine game of ball this morning and I am off tonight. This is a fine country down here. Elegant farms. We are getting along splendidly in our new home. Pearl put out her washing today and we are getting a new dining-room table. Our store is not far from this market and on Saturday they have large crowds. Owen Sound don't know what a good market means, ha-ha. Is T. still going with Miss C.? It will be good if someone ropes him in. Write soon. A. S.

"Marche Public, Marieville, Que."

"Have had lots of fun. You must let H. J. S. persuade you to come through this country."

The nineteenth-century city hall and market building were demolished in 1964.

Habitant Life

HABITANT LIFE IN EDWARDIAN QUEBEC focussed on a robust and happy family life. Rural families in Quebec have changed perhaps less than those in other parts of Canada, and family ties are still stronger than elsewhere in the country.

American tourists loved Quebec—and there were tourists, even in those days, marvelling at the grandeur of the Rockies, or the beauty of small Nova Scotian communities, or gawking at the old bake ovens, dog carts, and sturdy habitants of Quebec. And there is character indeed in the appearance of the habitant family, the gnarled, wiry men and the plump, firm-willed, and hard-working women.

We have a complete series of Edwardian cards that deal with gathering maple sap and boiling the syrup. In those days, it was a great industry in Quebec. In 1910, Quebec turned out more than 16.5 million pounds of maple sugar, three times as much as Ontario's production and forty times as much as the rest of the country combined. Maple syruping was much more than a pleasant jaunt to the woods on an early spring day.

Edwardian postals from Quebec villages, as these examples demonstrate, tend to be in black and white, with a soft diffused look that gave them, even in those days, a patina of the past.

The message reads: "Making rag carpet—I thought it was homespun at first but find it is not. . . ."

Boiling the Maple Sap.

Putting Maple Sugar into Moulds.

Felling the Timber

THE LUMBER INDUSTRY of the Edwardian period tends to be forgotten amidst the celebration of Canada as "the granary of the Empire." It is true that the production of wheat was on the increase and that of lumber declining, but, nevertheless, in 1912 the value of lumber cut in Canada was over $69 million and that of wheat just over $138 million. In other words, lumbering was still big business; it brought in half as much money as did wheat and a good many men made their living out of the woods.

Lumbering in British Columbia was next in importance to mining. Red cedar shingles were marketed as far east as Ontario and the beautiful grains of B.C. fir made it very popular as a finishing wood throughout Canada and the northwestern United States.

The Ottawa Valley was another famous lumber producer; in fact, for a hundred years, ending in 1909, the lumber industry was the most important feature of life in the valley. To see a raft of squared timber arrive at Quebec City was a sight indeed. It might contain close to 2,000 pieces of squared timber. And it might take from April till July for that raft to complete its journey, beginning in the tributaries of the Ottawa as single pieces, then joining smaller units at the mouth of the Ottawa, through rapids and down slides, and finally forming a gigantic raft in the latter part of the trip.

The early cards of lumbering are fascinating. The physical effort demanded of man and horse is beyond our powers to comprehend. We have a card of a lumberjack perched precariously on a log during a river drive and on the back of the card is printed this information, capturing the flavour of the time:

The lumberjack. A cheery careless soul; daily dangers, hard living make his occasional visits to civilization, as a rule, somewhat riotous and strenuous. He is always glad to get back to the woods again. Recruited from many nations, the freemasonry of the bush breeds a strong comradeship despite differences in language, creeds, and customs.

Near St. John's, Nfld.

Tully's Saw Mill, New Glasgow, N.S.

Lumbermen and railroaders used to say there were three cooks in every camp—one there, one going, and one coming.

Lumbering was the main factor in the economic life of the Ottawa Valley from 1806 until the last crib went through in 1909.

Latchford is in the Nipissing area of northern Ontario.

Logs were steered from the Sturgeon River country down the Shell and Red rivers into the North Saskatchewan River when breakup came.

Working the Mines

SCATTERED ACROSS THE COUNTRY were small flax mills, sulphite plants, and limestone quarries that were the lifeblood of local communities, and as such were justly considered worthy of the photographer's eye.

Our cards show a few of the larger industries, such as the towering coal colliery at Glace Bay, Nova Scotia, and the Johnson Asbestos Works at Thetford Mines, Quebec. Asbestos mining began at Thetford in 1881, and was well-established by the turn of the century.

There is a unique card showing the troops marching through the streets of Springhill, Nova Scotia, to quell the miners' strike of 1909-11.

It was the mining fields of northern Ontario that sparked the most intense excitement during these years. On September 15, 1903, a big-bellied, moon-faced man, Fred La Rose, strolled into Noah Timmins' store in Mattawa, carrying a little canvas bag of rocks. The rocks contained silver and it was La Rose's discovery that launched the great silver rush and spelled prosperity for Cobalt and Haileybury.

The feverish activity is evident in this card from Cobalt, Ont.: Tuesday Evening, September 1, 1908, 10 o'clock P.M. "This place is immensely fascinating tonight. Bush fires are raging on some of the hills about us. The Mines are all working nights too and most of them are lit electrically and the effect is really fine. The Fire Brigades are kept busy though. Elias."

The first oil towns established in Canada were Oil Springs and Petrolia, both in Ontario. Between 1857 and 1876 these towns flourished as nearby shallow wells brought black crude to the surface. Ontario oil companies even exported to Europe (kerosene was the main product), but about 1876 the price plunged from one dollar to twelve cents a gallon, and the oil bubble burst.

Imperial Oil was founded in 1880 with headquarters at Petrolia. In 1898 the company laid a pipeline from Petrolia to Sarnia where its refinery produced 900 barrels a day.

Part of this domestic production supported the growing automobile industry. There were 178 cars in Canada in 1903 and 5,890 by 1910. Early motorists bought gasoline in cans from grocery or hardware stores, but inevitably gas stations sprang up. The first gas pump in Canada was installed in 1907 at Smythe and Cambie streets in Vancouver.

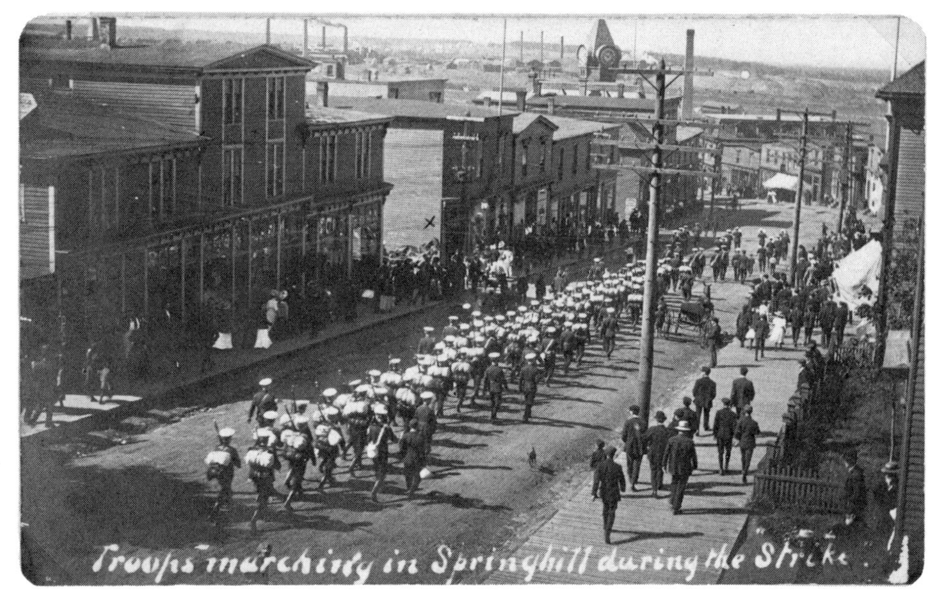

"Troops marching in Springhill during the strike."

Cobalt, January 21, 1907: "Dear Amy—I thought you were the girl who was going to write to me. Heard you were lonesome for a few days—don't take it so bad, wifie. . . ."

At work at Nipissing Mines, Cobalt, Ont.

At one time there were twenty-three operating coal mines in the Edmonton area.

August 7, 1905: "Arrived here last night. Spent one day at Calgary, two days at Banff, a delightful place & the trip through the Rockies beyond description. Leave for Vancouver tomorrow. T. S. F."

The Klondike

SO MANY AMERICANS poured into the Yukon on the trail of '98 that there are actually cards labelled "Dawson City, Alaska"; indeed, a card in this section refers to the gold rush in Alaska. Gold rush cards were mailed throughout the Edwardian period showing scenes from the days of '98 but these cards are now very scarce.

The indomitable Martha Black went over the Chilkoot Pass to Dawson. She described it vividly:

I looked up the Pass. I can see it yet—that upward trail outlined on an almost perpendicular wall of ice-covered rock, alive with clinging human beings and animals, slowly mounting, single file to the summit. . . . We clung to stunted pines, spruce roots, jutting rocks. In some places the path was so narrow that to move at all we had to use our feet tandem fashion. Above, only the granite wall; below, death leering at us. At one moment, there were the screams of pack horses, too heavily loaded, which lost their footing and were dashed to the rocks below.

Dawson boasted a very cosmopolitan population, even after the heady days of the gold rush. For instance, this message to Kingston, Ont., from Dawson, November 30, 1910: "Delighted on receiving your card from Old England. How did you enjoy your stay over there—that part of England is quite a winter resort, isn't it? . . . We are enjoying some pretty cold weather now but very moderate for this time of year. We have some great skating though for a considerable part of the year, in fact far too long a period to suit me."

A bird's-eye view of Dawson bears this comment: August 11, 1910: "Dear friend—This is a picture of the town where we live. It is a typical mining town. It has a population of about 3,000 at present, but the population is decreasing yearly."

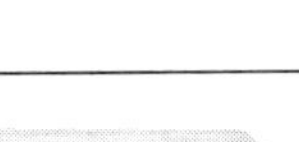

It cost one dollar to send a letter from Dawson to Skagway.

Boats of the Northern Commercial Company. The lower Yukon boats ran between Dawson and St. Michael on the Alaska coast.

The Klondike Mines Railway ran approximately 12 miles through the gold-mining country from Dawson City ("Lousetown") to Bonanza or "The Forks".

Dawson was named for the colourful Canadian geologist George M. Dawson.

The Chilkoot Pass was so steep, it was a veritable death trap. Note the erroneous claim of the caption writer: "the gold rush in Alaska".

Dance-hall girls became famous: Montreal Marie, Lime Juice Lil, Diamond-Tooth Gertie, and a teenaged dancer who called herself Klondike Kate.

This ornate mansion was destroyed by fire on Christmas Day, 1906.

Baedeker's Canada for 1907 reports: "Britannia has a popular park, with a good bathing-beach, boating, a long pier, band-concerts, and vaudeville performances."

This Sunday service started back in the late 1880s and still continues to this day.

Regina, Sask.: "Howdy, May—Why don't you take a trip to this growing west? Alf."

View from Mowat Island, near Parry Sound, Georgian Bay, Canada

HOUSE BOATING
ON GEORGIAN BAY, CANADA
2089 S

Love's Greeting.

Angelo Asti was a French artist who died in 1903. His lush, Rembrandt-style portraits of women were delicately reproduced on Edwardian postcards. →

GERMANS ICELANDERS SCOTCHMEN ENGLISHMEN AMERICANS FRENCHMEN SCANDINAVIANS
BELGIANS RUSSIANS AUSTRIANS IRISHMEN
THE MAPLE LEAF FOR EVER
CANADA
"NOW THEN, ALL TOGETHER"
Serie No. 900 THE NATIONAL SONG OF CANADA

C.T. Howard
The Maple Leaf our emblem dear,
The Maple Leaf for ever;
God save our King, and Heaven bless
The Maple Leaf for ever.

THE
MAPLE LEAF
FOR EVER
Best
Wishes

CANADA
Flags of the Nations' Series

BEST WISHES
FROM CANADA
Macdonald Range
Three Sisters
Cathedral Peak
Mount "Sir Donald"
THE ROCKY MOUNTAINS

HIS MAJESTY KING EDWARD VII.
"Oilette"

FRED^K SPURGIN
WE CAN HOLD OUR OWN.

CANADA.
HIS EXCELLENCY, THE GOVERNOR GENERAL EARL GREY
LADY GREY.
LORD STRATHCONA
RT HON. SIR JOHN A MACDONALD
RT HON. SIR WILFRED LAURIER.

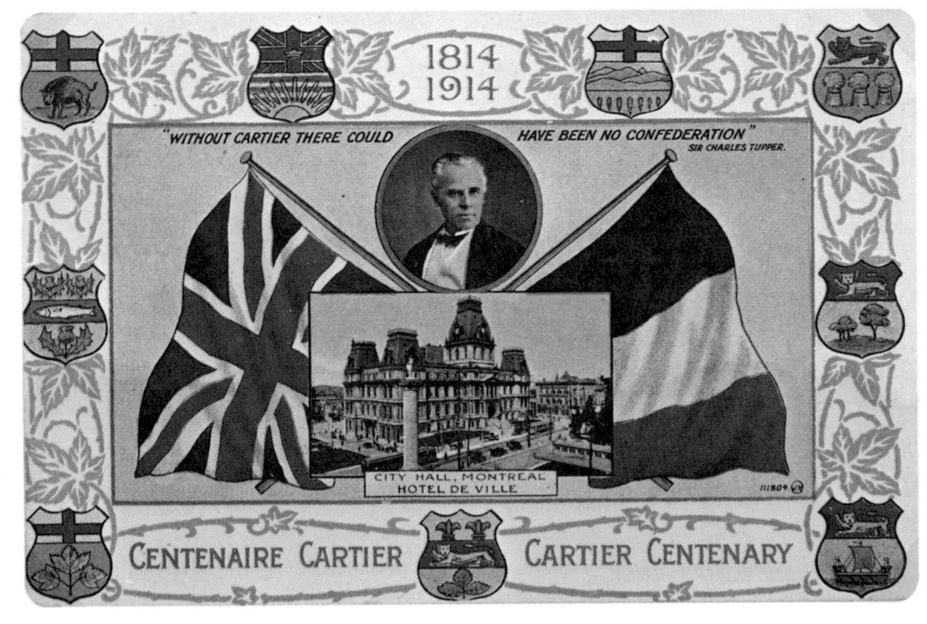
1814
1914
"WITHOUT CARTIER THERE COULD HAVE BEEN NO CONFEDERATION"
SIR CHARLES TUPPER.
CITY HALL, MONTREAL
HOTEL DE VILLE
CENTENAIRE CARTIER
CARTIER CENTENARY

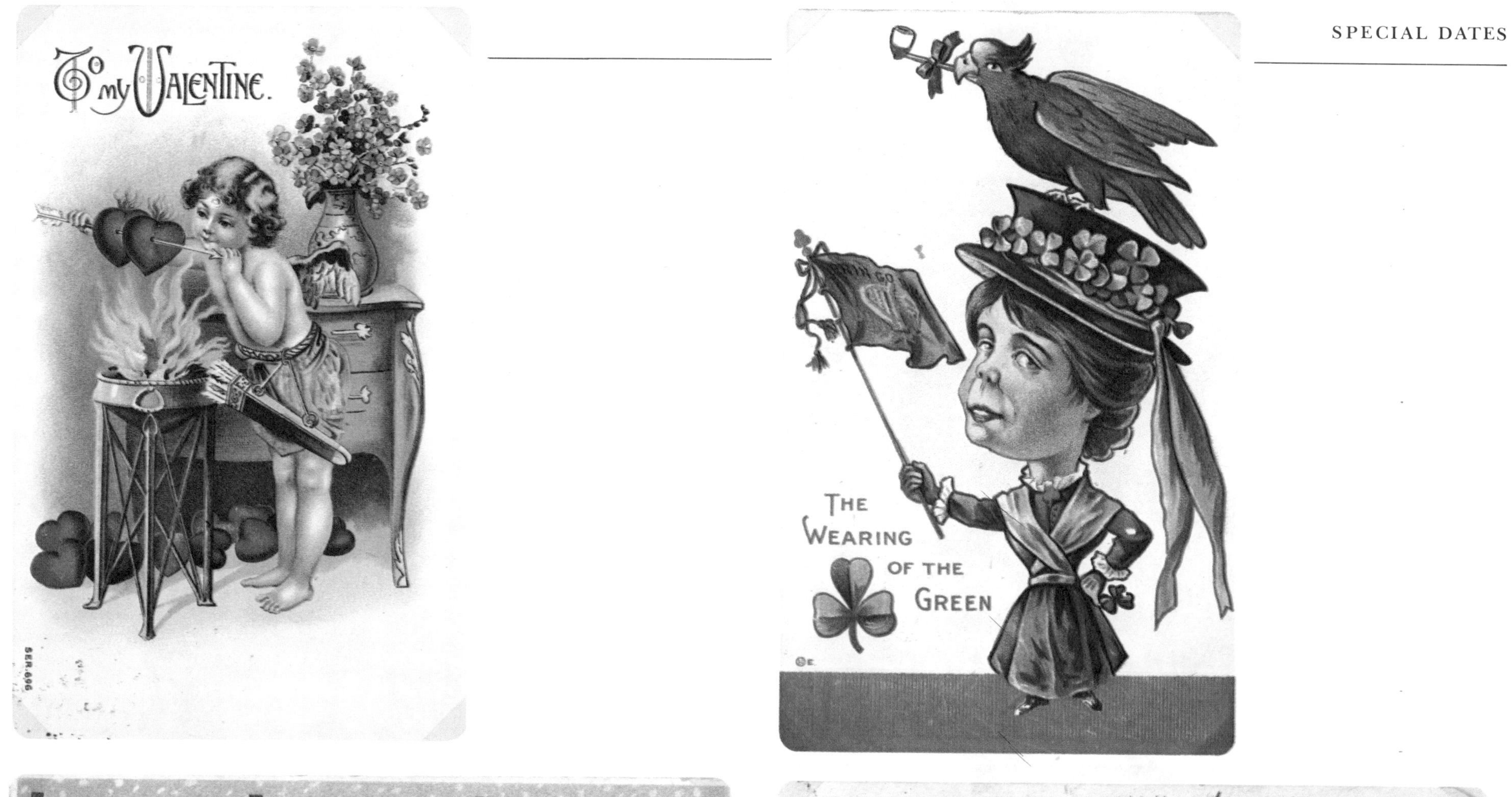
To my Valentine.
The Wearing of the Green

A Joyous Easter

OCT
31
YOU AUTO HAVE A
HAPPY HALLOWE'EN

May 24th
Victoria Day in Canada

A merry Christmas
842

Sluicing gold in the Klondike.

Days of Sail

MANY A THREE-MASTED SCHOONER was launched from the small shipyards of such places as Saint John, New Brunswick, which had been turning out ships for generations. The men who built and designed these sailing vessels were master craftsmen; the tradition was honorable and enduring. Except for one or two large vessels built during the First World War, all the schooners were designed by the shipbuilders themselves; there were no blueprints or calculated sail plans used.

The schooners had two drawbacks. They were built mostly of soft wood—only some of the fastenings, chain plates, and anchor gear were iron—and after a decade or so, it didn't pay to repair them. Second, they were dangerous, prey to the winds and the tides. More than one white-painted, three- or four-masted vessel ended up on the rocks or the beaches.

By 1910 Canada had 952 lighthouses under government control and had become a leader in lighthouse design. Each lighthouse had different markings and different signals to aid mariners. Until 1900, many Canadian lighthouses used "multiple wick" Doty burners that used cheap kerosene. The first electric filament lamps were introduced before the First World War.

A July 19, 1907, postcard shows the lighthouse at Manitowaning, Ontario, and a joking message reads: "Some light on matters marine."

SHIPPING AT MONTAGUE, P. E. ISLAND. "A BUSY DAY".

"COAL DOCK, PORT BOWMANVILLE, ONT."

Along the water front Lunenburg N. S.

La Have River near Bridgewater N. S.

Beacon Light, Yarmouth, N.S.

Lighthouse, Port Stanley Ont., Canada

Baccalieu Island Lighthouse.
The land on which this light is situated is said to be the first sighted by Guy.

GEORGINA POINT, ACTIVE PASS, B.C.

Harvesting the Sea

IN 1908, fishing brought in only about one-quarter of the money wheat farming did, but it was still a $25 million business. In that year, dried cod, preserved lobster, and preserved salmon were big sellers. By 1912-13, there were 88,000 fishermen in Canada, and canned salmon, as it was called by then, was the major item—$7 million worth of it was sold, and the total take from fishing had risen to $33 million.

Fishing was a hard but to many an exotic occupation. People enjoyed visiting the canneries. One postcard shows 50,000 salmon at a plant in New Westminster, B.C., and the 1910 message reads: "Don't you try to eat up all the fish on this card, or it will be worse than too much 'ham', ha-ha."

Another message is from Steveston, B.C., where the inhabitants were mostly Japanese fishermen, and it is a laconic comment: August 5, 1909: "Spending the day here. Just been in the canneries. Lots of fish."

"Quebec—
The Turbot
salting house."

Steamboat Round the Bend

IN 1907, there were more steamship and steamboat lines in operation in Canada than there were railways. Over 60 different railways travelled back and forth across the country, but more than 75 steamship and steamboat lines were busy on the lakes and rivers. The lonely whistle of the steamers rivalled the long wailing of the locomotives in the minds of many Edwardians.

The *Canadian Almanac* of 1907 warns travellers: "Inasmuch as steamboat lines are not fixed as are railroads but are constantly changing, this list must be used by shippers and travellers with caution." It points out that winter conditions and low water can interrupt service and there follow four columns of listed steamboat lines. Among them are the Restigouche and Bonaventure steam ferries, which went from Dalhousie to Campbellton, New Brunswick; Dobell's Line, from Montreal to St. John's, Newfoundland; Rainy Lake Steamboat, connecting at Fort Frances, Ontario, with the steamboat for Rat Portage, Ontario; the CPR's Okanagan Lake route between Okanagan Landing and Penticton, British Columbia; and the New Westminster and Chilliwack steamer route in British Columbia.

Edwardians loved watching boats, meeting boats, and sometimes they enjoyed travelling on them.

Burlington, Ont.: "My it is lovely sitting out on the verandas of Brant House overlooking the lake and watching the boats and all sorts of things and not having to prepare meals."

Yarmouth, N.S., August 11, 1906: "The trip was fine but rough. Ellie and I succumbed but feel fine here. Our friends are alive and one is so talkative. Wish you were here. Alicia."

This message appears on a card showing the steamer *Prescott* running the Lachine rapids near Montreal: August 27, 1908: "This is not the boat we are in, but we went through these rapids. We were down to St. Anne de Beaupré today and Montmorency Falls and all over Quebec to see the places of interest. From Elsie."

The horrors of winter on the Great Lakes are recalled by a correspondent writing from Sarnia, Ont., December 7, 1905: "The lake boats are having a terrible time with storms, and come into the river all over ice and snow. Some snow here, not much yet. Madge."

Finally, this sour note from the Muskokas. Bala, Ont., August 15, 1907: "We are having a nice time here. Tomorrow we go on a trip up the lakes. Do not think there is any place you would care for around here, as there is not much fishing and every place is crowded. Weighed this morning 119 pounds. D. M. H." The Edwardians had a compulsive need to reveal to each other their exact weights—maybe their friends kept wall charts!

"Alice—If you and your mother can quilt this quilt next spring I will settle with you. . . . Ada."

There was fog on the St. Lawrence when the Norwegian collier *Storstad* rammed the CPR's *Empress of Ireland*, May 29, 1914. She sank in fifteen minutes and over a thousand died.

The Richelieu and Ontario Navigation Company ran its Saguenay Line two to four times a week between Quebec City and Chicoutimi.

One of the most popular of the Ontario lake steamers, the *Cayuga* served superb meals, including fresh lake trout.

"Sail on this boat to Killarney. Sixty miles on such a tub. Cliff." Killarney is a northern Ontario community.

The Huntsville and Lake of Bays Navigation Company provided service three to six times a week from Huntsville in the Muskokas.

This lock opened for traffic in 1910 to by-pass rapids on the Red River, fifteen miles north of Winnipeg.

The *Marquis* and her sister ship the *Northcote* were pressed into service during the Riel Rebellion of 1885 to carry troops and supplies.

The *Inlander* was the last commercial ship on the Skeena. She had such a shallow draft, she could float on "anything a trifle moist".

Isolated prospectors and trappers, eagerly awaiting supplies — especially liquor—swore they could hear the whistle of the *Kokanee* for twenty miles.

Nakusp took a half-holiday when the CPR launched the S.S. *Bonnington* on April 24, 1911. She was the biggest sternwheeler of her day north of San Francisco.

This 250-passenger vessel was launched in B.C. in 1907, when business with settlers was booming. She boasted a handsome dining room and cabins finished in gold and enamel.

The Iron Horse

In Canada in 1907 the railways practically ran all over each other. The CPR alone had about 88 branch lines and the Grand Trunk 59. There were railways most Canadians had never heard of: the Halifax and Yarmouth in Nova Scotia; the Canada Eastern in New Brunswick, the Carillon and Granville in Quebec, the Bay of Quinte Railway in Ontario; and the Kaslo and Slocan in British Columbia.

Edwardians happily scribbled messages to each other about the pleasures and agonies of train travel. From New Glasgow, N.S. to St. Agatha, Ont.: "Thought I would send you a card from Nova Scotia, a long way from home. Yesterday our train ran off the track in a bad place and it took almost a day to rebuild the road and get the train in motion; nobody hurt."

Here are words of advice for a new arrival in Canada: "My dear May—Welcome to Canada. Hope you had a pleasant voyage. Don't forget what I told you about the boxes at Quebec, get them checked, keep the duplicate, and don't worry after that. If you haven't enough to eat, be sure and get something there, and don't forget to wire from Montreal, whether you are coming Canadian Pacific or Grand Trunk Railway, and what time you are leaving, it will cost 25¢ for ten words. With love from Fred."

Toronto, Ont., January 10, 1909: "I got in here this morning . . . we had a slow trip all the way down, the engine would freeze right up."

An early card dated March 10, 1904, from Winnipeg reads: "The rocky shores of Lake Superior were wonderful, though I should not care to get out just there in March. I slept three times during two nights at ten minutes a time. There is no Mendles'n Lieder to lull one to slumber, only jolts—jumps—screech — whistle in regular altercations and as a 'canon' the occasional wait at a station."

There was trouble on the track: "We have passed Brandon and going along at a good rate 14 cars on a very heavy train. We are about 5 hours behind, wreck on track last night kept us back, three passenger trains held up. . . ."

However there were compensations: Moose Jaw, January 12, 1907: "Nearly four hours late now. Very heavy train. Had some good games at whist. Remember me to all. 40 degrees below."

From Innisfail, Alta., to Clinton, Ont., August 2, 1910: "We are enjoying the trip very much, are about 3,000 miles from home now, but it does not seem that far."

To Sackville, N.B.: "Tonight is our last on the train & I am thankful. Yesterday the heat was terrible in the train, the prairies were on fire, a lot of grain burning. An awful day!"

Into the mountains in bad weather: "We are getting later all the time, not passed Glacier yet, lots of snow slides and delays due to heavy snow. Have spent all the time out on the observation car."

And a final note from Vancouver, August 28, 1907: "Dear Mabel—I arrived here yesterday and have had a fine trip. I had my hand read and fortune told by cards by a lady on the train. Oh joy. Clarence."

"Carillon and Granville Rly. Train; Oldest train in America." This Quebec railway was still running in Edwardian times.

Baedeker's Canada of 1907 reports: "The 'Flying Bluenose' express leaves Halifax daily at 8:30 A.M. The railway is well equipped, and its officials are notably courteous."

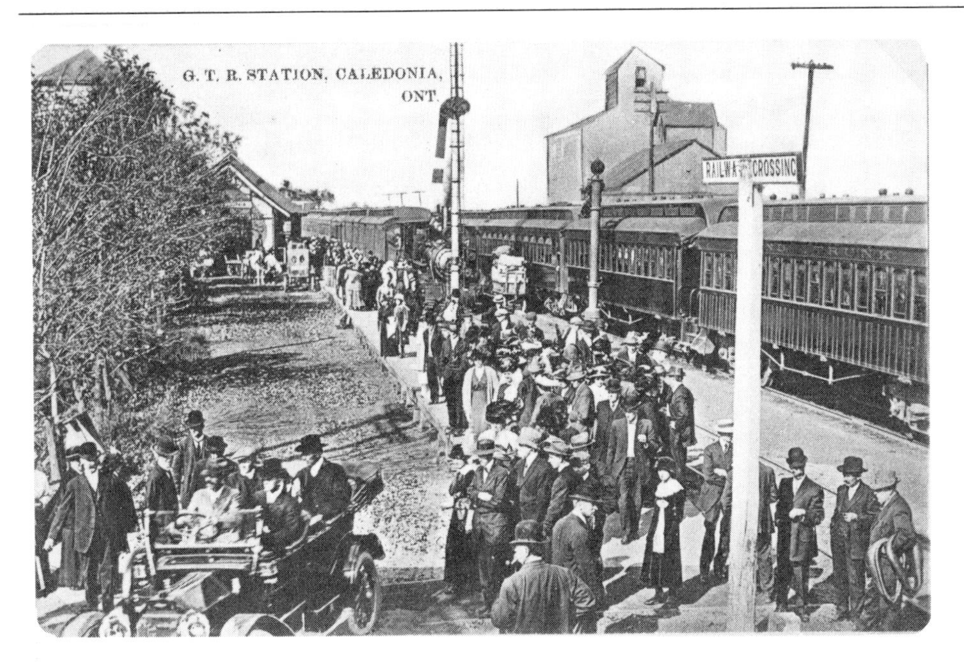

The Grand Trunk Railway, incorporated in 1853, was for many years the chief railway system in Ontario and Quebec.

"We had the best coach on the train. Ten school teachers on it. The train was crowded with them."

The first Grand Trunk Pacific train to leave Winnipeg arrived at its western terminus, Prince Rupert, April 9, 1914.

The curves on the Phoenix section of the CPR were "so sharp that the fireman, when throwing coal in the firebox, often hit the engine in the headlight."

On the notorious Caledon horseshoe curve, about fifty miles northwest of Toronto, a Canadian National Exhibition Special went roaring off the track. Seven passengers were killed and many injured.

"Harvest Special Smashed by the Eastbound Express. Brakes Refused to Work" reported the Toronto *Globe* about this Ontario wreck that claimed seven lives.

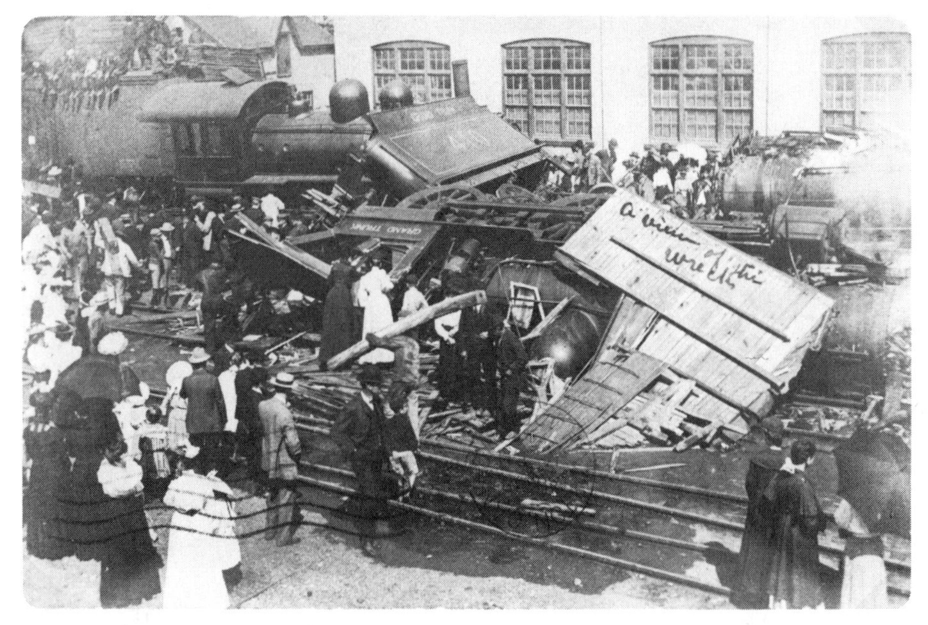

Port Arthur, Ont.: "This happened right here at the station."

"Wreck on CPR at Tottenham, June 27, 1908." No lives were lost in this mishap. Local residents still recall picking up souvenirs from the overturned cars.

Bird's-Eye Views

A view of Fogo, Nfld.

Every village, town, and city boasted a bird's-eye view of itself taken by an agile photographer who got up in a church steeple or climbed a water tower, or, if he was lucky, simply walked to the top of the nearest hill.

While bird's-eye views are bound to have a certain similarity, they are fascinating because they show the look of a community at a certain stage in its growth (or decline). Bird's-eye views—and they were never called anything else — of western communities taken, perhaps, two or three years apart, illustrate vividly the way in which the West mushroomed.

It seems unusually difficult to find bird's-eye views of certain places. There are all kinds of shots of the harbour of St. John's, Newfoundland, but it took years to locate a genuine bird's-eye view of the entire city of St. John's.

Viewers of these cards today will puzzle over what part of the community they are looking at in relation to its current boundaries.

Treherne is in Manitoba, but evidently some of its early residents were from Ontario.

"We are in the land of the Cowboys. It is going along amazing, there were only about 20,000 people last year, now there are 45,000 and more coming; buildings going up in all directions!"

Full of roistering prospectors in its early years, this mining community in the Kootenays provided everything from prize fights to boa-feathered dance-hall girls.

The Big City

By 1911, THE NUMBER OF PEOPLE in urban Canada had almost caught up with the rural population. A significant fact is that, in the decade between 1901 and 1911, the rural population increased by only 17 per cent while the urban population shot up by 62 per cent. Of the seventeen cities shown in this section of the book, only one dropped in population during the period: Charlottetown had 82 fewer people in 1911 than in 1901. Other Maritime cities showed modest increases. Montreal's population very nearly doubled: in 1911 it was 470,500. Toronto's increase was smaller but still impressive—an 80 per cent increase to 376,000. Most impressive of all, however, was the growth in Western Canada. Saskatoon could only round up 113 people in 1901, but it had 12,000 in 1911. Regina increased 14 times to 30,000, Calgary 10 times to 44,000.

There is abundant evidence of the long hours worked by city dwellers.

Halifax, N.S., September 13, 1907: "I have just arrived home from the store and it is after 10."

Another comment: "I go to work at 8 o'clock or 8:15 and work till 6:30 every night nearly."

Incidentally, the cedar poles used by telephone and telegraph companies in cites and towns during the first half of the Edwardian period were in the main quite tall—26 to 30 feet high and up to 41 feet high. After about 1909, the poles were shorter—20 to 25 feet in height. It's possible to date an unmailed card by the size of the poles on the streets.

Now a glimpse of some Canadian cities through Edwardian eyes.

Halifax

"This sure is a good town. Having a fine time."

July 9, 1913: "Glad to hear you are a little better. We are filled up with teachers for the summer school of science."

"I may go downtown tomorrow, if not too cold. I hope you will get out and have a sleigh ride."

Quebec City

September 15, 1910: "Arrived here all safe and sound. It is the most wonderful city. It is all up and down hill. The streets are very narrow. The city is full of sightseers."

July 31, 1906: "Curious old town, narrow crooked streets named for the saints. French is spoken everywhere. Soldiers, nuns, and friars in evidence."

October 3, 1908: "Montreal was very nice, but Quebec was too dirty to live in for me."

Montreal

This is a comment by an American visitor: August 25, 1906: "This is a dirty city and a dirty looking people all jabbing French."

March 18, 1910: "I go to Montreal for the company as assistant to the Manager. How is that for travelling some?"

Ottawa

March 3, 1912: "Hello, sister—Just a line to let you know that I am in Ottawa and was at the fastest game of hockey played this year. Quebec and Ottawa. Quebec beating them by one goal. This is some city, am going to see the parliament buildings this afternoon. Goodbye from Alf."

From Ottawa, Ont., to Perth, July 22, 1914: "Dear Helen—A card from Robin. He says Ottawa is grand. He likes the cars & ice cream. We think this a lovely place."

Toronto

To Grace in Victoria, B.C., from Lottie in Toronto, April 9, 1908: "This is the place that I try to be good in once a week."

"Am having a fine time. This is certainly a beautiful city. Nothing like it in Pennsylvania."

Another card to the States, this one from Beckie to her cousin Minnie, August 11, 1906: "I don't believe you can have a good time any place else but Toronto so take the first car you see and come here."

And a contrary opinion: "We are going to rubber around Toronto for a while. This is a busy and dirty place."

To Paris, Ont., from Ingersoll, September 8, 1908: "I was down to Toronto last week to the Exhibition and the excitement was too much for me."

Toronto to Wiarton, Ont., February 11, 1907: "I think they have made some mistake here, for Sunday comes too often and stays too long."

Hamilton

This message appears on the back of a card dated October 21, 1907, which shows the Hamilton Tigers Football Team and identifies the players: "The Tigers won in Montreal this afternoon 9 to 7 not much points to win by, but still they won."

Winnipeg

August 27, 1911: "This is the prettiest city west of Sudbury. It has got B. skinned a mile. It has such nice wide streets and well paved, good streetcars."

July 28, 1905: "Dear Brother—Arrived at Winnipeg at last

and I am beginning to like this city fairly well. We have a fine store here and the people are very friendly. I have some idea of what you felt like last winter in Toronto. Well, cheer up, I think I will have 'a small cup of tea.' Sister Robbie."

November 3, 1911: "You ought to see the little girls here in wolfskin with ears standing up on the caps of fur. They are cunning, helpless bundles trying to keep the cold out from their tender little limbs."

To Laura in Cranbrook, B.C., from Addie, September 1, 1904: "This is the main street and it is the widest street I ever saw. There are two streetcar tracks on it and the cars are running both ways all the time."

October 22, 1912: "Winnie—We arrived safely at 2 A.M. yesterday. Mr. B. met us along with a friend, so he and Mrs. H. were with us when we were married by Ralph Connor; was sick all the way out. . . ."

Winnipeg to Toronto, May 10, 1912: "Just got in here and from first impressions it looks like a fine city. It seems funny to me to think I am here some way or other. It seems so far away from Toronto. . . ."

Regina

July 3, 1914: "Plenty of rain and mud here. Had a pleasant drive over the prairie yesterday afternoon. Going again tomorrow and to a picnic this afternoon. Sifton's to tea. They all have potatoes in their front lawns. . . ."

"Have been enjoying delightful times at Regina Beach. Just got home."

Calgary

July 20, 1912: "Dear Mother—Wish you were here. This place has Brantford beaten to a frazzle. Wish you could see the flowers and the grass. . . ."

May 10, 1910: "McIntyre struck town about 6 this A.M. and has been transferred to the Calgary office of the CPR. Wages $50 a month. Hardly think he will amount to much. Came right up to the house and pulled me out of bed. CPR always pays badly, and is the Englishman's home when he first comes out, and before he learns better. Business good."

"It is some dusty here and there are very few shade trees. . . ."

March 2, 1911: "You should come West. The only country on earth and Calgary the finest city in Canada. Like the West very much and have good position. No more East for me."

And this cryptic note: "Lizzie and boy are on my trail. Yours, Al."

Edmonton

"Glad to say we are safe at last in Edmonton. The worst has got to come yet and that is unpacking the goods, etc. Mother likes it very much up here and I am sure we shall all be much better when we get settled down. . . ."

"I hunted up Miss R. the very night I came up. She said she and Miss C. would call on me here. They are rooming together so if you want to come up you will have a good time. I think she is a nice little girl. Your Aunty."

"This is the prettiest city in Alberta—after Banff."

Vancouver

August 27, 1909: "John:—This is a hustling city and quite a sight to one who has never seen the ocean. Paul."

March 22, 1915: "This is some climate out here. The grass is green and the boys don't wear any overcoats. They had no snow this winter. Horace."

July 10, 1910: "Have been house hunting this last week. The houses here are hard to find empty."

June 24, 1908: "We have just been around the city and Stanley Park in a Tally-Ho. We are staying at the Vancouver Hotel. Rates $4 per day. Having an excellent time."

June 24, 1911: "I am in love with Vancouver. The mountains are so beautiful. We have had the loveliest excursions to beauty spots near Vancouver and launch rides on the bay. Coronation day was a big one here, immense parades."

Victoria

From Helen to Hazel in Toronto: "I hope you have your husband home by now, and that you are all well and happy again. I am having a grand time in this lovely seacoast city and feeling so well, and getting so fat. . . ."

A message about the Empress Hotel, October 8, 1909: "This is certainly the gem of the CPR hotels. We are having a jolly little trip without cousins. . . ."

"This is where we were lying. Isn't it a hilly place? G. S."

The oldest street in North America. The land was claimed for Elizabeth I in 1583.

Sent to Canning, N.S., June 2, 1905.

Hotel Victoria, Charlottetown, P.E.I., 1908.

One of the earliest cards in the collection.

South Park Street, Halifax, N.S.

Queen Victoria's father, the Duke of Kent, once lived with his mistress, Madame de St. Laurent, on an estate at Halifax. This was their music room, built in 1796.

Fredericton, N.B., November 3, 1913: "I am down here going to school, but examinations begin in two weeks and likely they will send me home then. Be sure and shiver for me. . . ."

In 1785 Saint John became British North America's first incorporated city. Most postcard captions incorrectly abbreviate the name to "St. John".

King Square, where the homeless citizens of Saint John slept in army tents after the devastating fire of June 1877.

Montreal, Que., April 8, 1910: "This is a peculiar place, wish you could see it. Am having some awful experiences. J. H. R."

St. Catherine Street (West), Montreal
GROCERIES
WINES

His Majesty's
RYAN
103,917
His Majesty's Theatre, Guy Street,
Montreal.

613 — MONTREAL. — A « Look Out » on Mont Royal.
MONTREAL. — Vue générale sur le Mont Royal. ND. Phot.

Observation Car, Montreal
104443

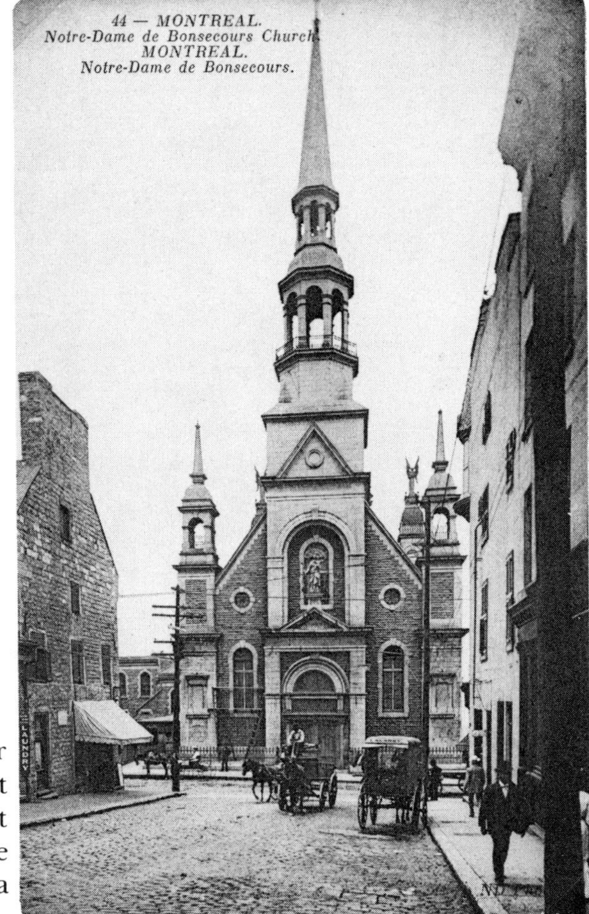

Twelve years after Donald Smith drove that famous last railway spike at Craigellachie, he was made a peer—Baron Strathcona and Mount Royal.

By Edwardian times Montreal winter carnivals were well-established. About 250,000 cubic feet of ice were cut from the St. Lawrence to make this magnificent palace.

"Dear Ma—I got my red suit for 96 cents and my waist for 48 cents, my hat for $1.25. I've got Maggie a waist and Pa a watch chain. Good-bye. Mary."

Robert Reed was a wealthy Saint John shipping merchant. The castle was partially burned in the 1890s and demolished in 1914.

An artist's brush transformed this daylight photo into a romantic night-time scene.

This is the earliest Canadian card in the collection; it is dated 1899.

The low building with the curved roof was Toronto's first large railway station, the Great Western. By the time this photo was taken it had become a wholesale fruit market.

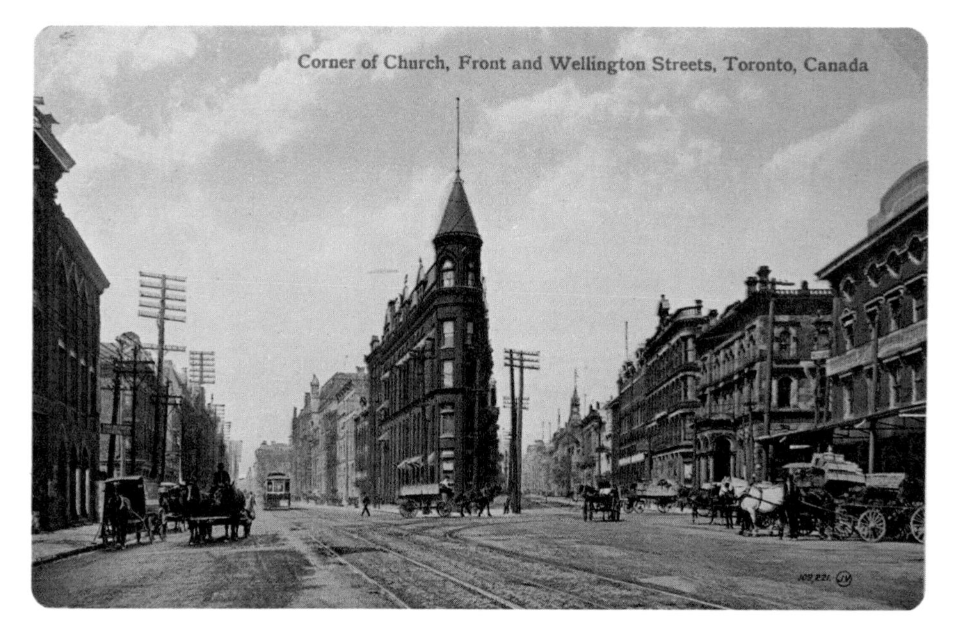

Toronto Ferry Boat "Bluebell" at Hanlans Point, Toronto

Water Scene near the Island, Toronto

12535—Gore Park,
Hamilton, Canada.
This
is at
the
Corner
of
King
and
James
Streets
Isn't it
pretty

Lover's Walk,
Ottawa.

As early as 1904, Winnipeg had an automobile club and held its first cross-country run. The club was the parent of the Manitoba Motor League.

This hotel was located directly across from the CPR station, jumping-off point for thousands of immigrants who were preyed upon mercilessly by shysters and shady ladies along Main Street.

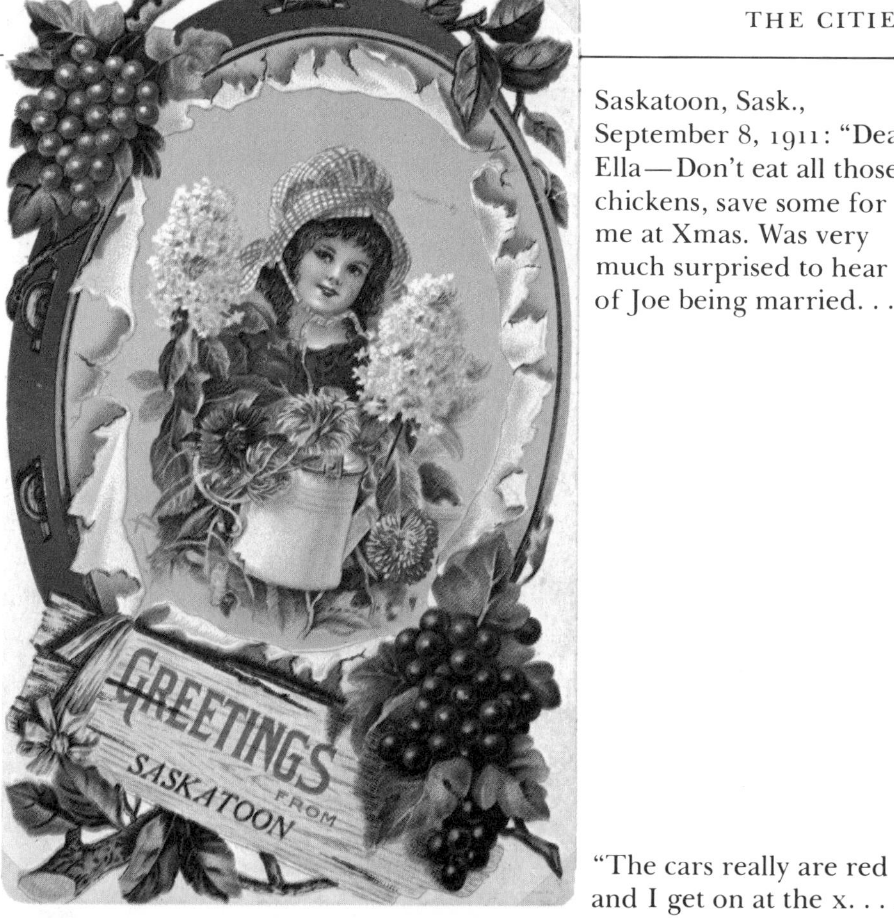

Saskatoon, Sask., September 8, 1911: "Dear Ella—Don't eat all those chickens, save some for me at Xmas. Was very much surprised to hear of Joe being married. . . ."

"The cars really are red and I get on at the x. . . ."

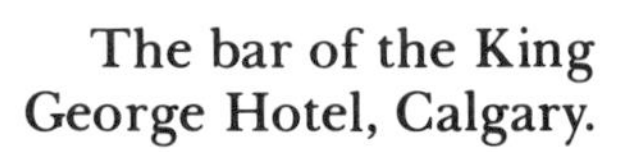
The bar of the King George Hotel, Calgary.

"We are here by auto. Bully time among the Canucks, don't yer know. . . ."

The first passenger train crossed the newly-opened High Level Bridge on June 2, 1913.

"Freight Scows bound for the North. . . ." Edmonton was the gateway to the North even then.

April 16, 1913: "Pioneers say never such a March in twenty-five years. However people are rolling and cutting their lawns and lots of flowers in bloom. . . ."

June 1908: "We have just been around the city and Stanley Park in a Tally-Ho. We are staying at the Vancouver Hotel, rates $4 per day."

"They say the trip past Victoria is every bit as beautiful as the Thousand Island trip. It certainly is fine. Aunt Minnie."

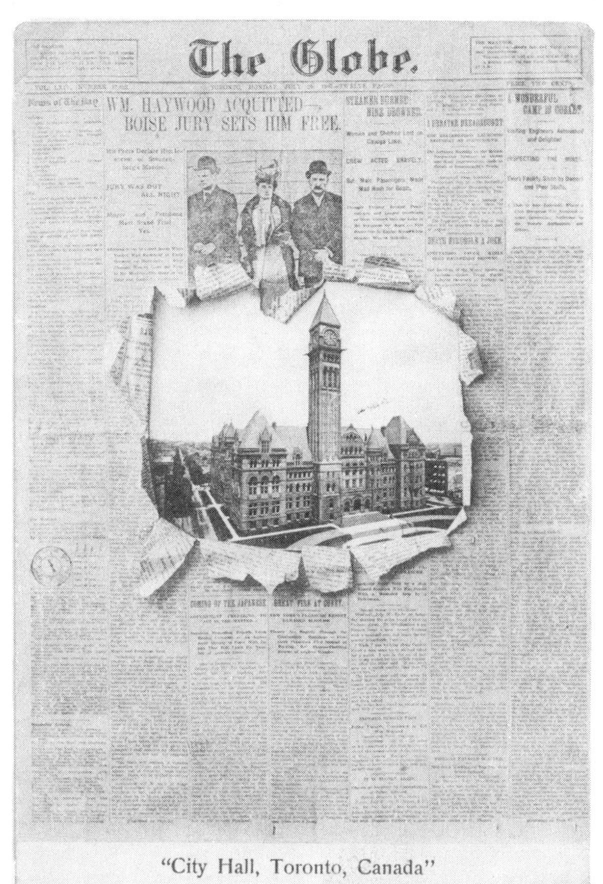

The Globe.

WM. HAYWOOD ACQUITTED—
BOISE JURY SETS HIM FREE.

JURY WAS OUT ALL NIGHT.

CREW ACTED BRAVELY.

"City Hall, Toronto, Canada"

The Globe's front page is dated July 29, 1907.

"Yonge Street, North from Richmond Street, Toronto, Canada." Note the open-sided streetcars.

Tea dances on the second floor, ice-cream sodas on the first. Those were the features of McConkey's restaurant where Mrs. McConkey held sway at her desk, her fingers sparkling with diamonds.

Bay St., showing City Hall and Temple Bldg., Toronto, Canada

King Street (West), near Yonge, Toronto

Circa 1880, this Front Street building first displayed huge paintings of famous world events. Petrie's machinery exhibit followed in later years. Next door is the old Union Station, a block away from its present location.

"How are you getting along? I spent two days in Toronto. I feel the effects yet."

The Varsity rugby team, *circa* 1908.

Lake Shore Road and Long Branch Car, Toronto, Canada

Radial service crept west from Toronto along Lakeshore Road after 1892. It took fourteen years for the line to be completed as far as Port Credit.

Could they have done this in Toronto?

The census for 1901 shows Hamilton with a population of 52,634. The view is an early one.

Though light-hearted, this card reveals something of the Edwardians' fascination with the aerial balloon.

Russell House is listed in *Baedeker's Canada* for 1907 at two and a half to four dollars a day, American plan (meals included).

The Queen's Restaurant, shown here at 15 Elgin Street, charged 25 cents for dinner.

This is an unusual "Hold to Light" card. The windows are illuminated when the card is held before a bright light.

In 1907 the Prime Minister of Canada was paid $12,000 a year, cabinet ministers received $7,000, senators and MP's $2,500.

This card, postmarked September 1905, shows the Royal Alexandra Hotel, at right, under construction.

"Winnipeg in fact has been rather given to the practice of announcing from the roof tops that she considers herself some potatoes." That quote comes from Winnipeg's newspaper, *Town Topics*, in 1902.

Waiting for the streetcar near Eaton's. By 1903 Winnipeg had "trolleys" tying the outlying areas to the centre of the community.

Troops were called out in Winnipeg during the 1906 railway strike. There were ugly scenes in which cars and company personnel were attacked.

The engine on display is the famed *Countess of Dufferin*, first railway engine in the Northwest. It arrived in Winnipeg in October 1877 on a barge, pushed down the Red River by the S.S. *Selkirk*.

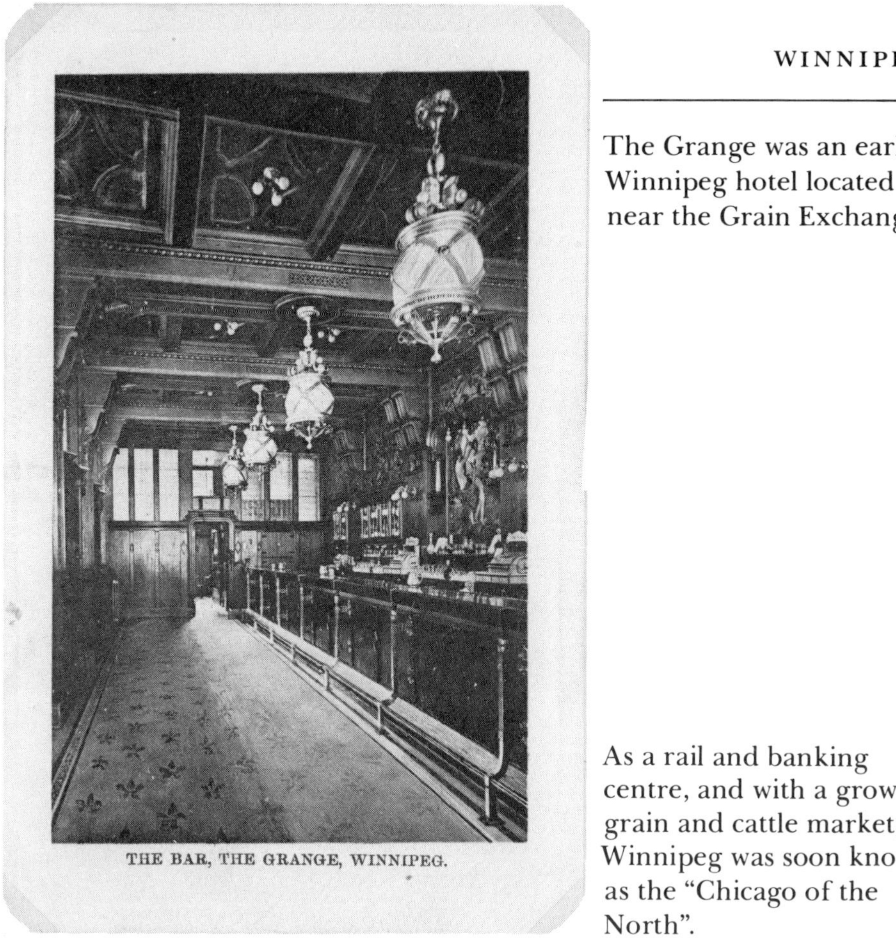

THE BAR, THE GRANGE, WINNIPEG.

The Grange was an early Winnipeg hotel located near the Grain Exchange.

As a rail and banking centre, and with a growing grain and cattle market, Winnipeg was soon known as the "Chicago of the North".

Regina's famous cyclone lasted just a few minutes on a stifling June afternoon in 1912. Twenty-eight people were killed, 2,500 left homeless, and property damage was estimated at over $4,000,000. Reconstruction was so speedy that within a year there was almost no sign of the disaster.

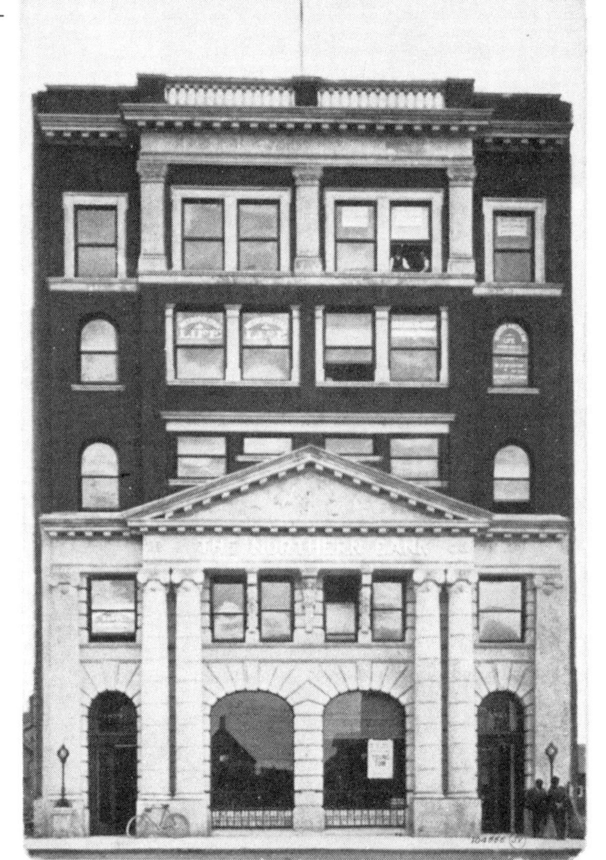

By May of 1907 an editorial in *The Leader* was urging enforcement of a by-law to control "furious driving". It said, "Does it not apply to automobiles speeding at twenty miles per hour equally to horses going ten or twelve?"

This early photocard of Saskatoon shows teams of horses at the ferry crossing.

A view of 21st Street looking towards the river where the Bessborough Hotel now stands.

Ferry service presented a perennial problem—high water and sandbars meant the ferry ran intermittently. The first traffic bridge opened in 1907, much to everyone's relief.

"Hoeschen Wentzley Brewing Co. Ltd., Saskatoon." The reverse side bears a stamped message: "Return empty kegs at once; we cannot ship beer without them."

Sir James Alexander Lougheed, born in Brampton, Ont., moved to Calgary in 1883. He became Conservative leader in the Senate in 1906 and from 1918-21 was minister of soldiers' civil re-establishment for Canada.

Evidently the American presence was felt in Calgary at an early date.

On May 24, 1913, the famous Luther McCarty of Chicago fought an unknown Calgary boxer, Arthur Pelkey, at the Manchester Arena. In the first round, after a few light blows, McCarty reeled back, collapsed, and died. Only thirty-six hours after the bout, the Manchester Arena mysteriously burned to the ground. Pelkey was charged with manslaughter, but was later acquitted. There is a story that McCarty had fallen off a horse the day before the fight. The tragedy shocked Calgarians, and boxing never regained the popularity it once enjoyed in that city.

July 4, 1906: "This will give you an idea of a small part of the town. . . ."

In 1911 an Edmonton lawyer wrote, "I'm sub-dividing my farm—it's halfway between Edmonton and St. Albert. I haven't decided whether to make it a suburb of Edmonton or St. Albert."

"Whyte Avenue, Edmonton South, Alta.", formerly Strathcona.

South Road, Edmonton, Alberta

"There are tents outside the Town, with Red-Lights, where lots of men go —I feel I can find lots better ways of wasting my hard earned money."

The Past and Present, Edmonton, Canada.

October 3, 1911: "The old fort stands just as shown on the other side. History lessons of childhood days, the Indians trading at Edmonton. . . ."

Post Office. Edmonton. Alta.

Edmonton, Alta., August 21, 1914: "Dear Josie: What is the matter with you? I haven't heard from you since last Saturday. . . . Ans. soon, Ray."

Hotel rates at Edmonton in 1908 averaged $1.50 to $3.00 a day.

Rotunda, Hotel Cecil, Edmonton, Alta.

North Vancouver. In the fall of 1909 lots overlooking Burrard Inlet sold for as little as $100.00—$5.00 down and $5.00 a month.

"Broadway after the Rainstorm, November 28, 1909."

Streetcars were very popular in Vancouver. They ran every five minutes and the fare was five cents.

"Listening to the Band, Stanley Park, Vancouver, B.C."

Everyone, but everyone, had his picture taken at the famous Big Tree in Stanley Park, so why not a wedding party as well?

"Capilano Suspension Bridge. Length 450 ft., Height above water 140 ft."

An early Robson streetcar, bearing an ad for the British Columbia Boxing Championship to be held at the Vancouver Athletic Club.

March 7, 1905: "Greetings from this quaint old English town."

An American visitor sent this message: "This is a great country; feel like a bloody Englishman and all that."

This was the first street in Victoria to have large stores. Traffic was English style, drivers keeping to the left.

Gorge Park in Victoria was as popular in Edwardian times as Beacon Hill.

"We are at a loss to know which we have most enjoyed, prairies, mountains, or sea, all are so wonderful. The gardens are full of roses, and sweet peas (7 or 8 feet long). It is marvelous how things grow here."

The Retail Trade

Interior Pearson's. Books, Stationery & Wall Paper, — House — Calgary.

THE EDWARDIANS eagerly embraced commerce and industry, but justifiably resented the long hours behind the counter or at the work table.

"Am working late every night, will send a letter as soon as I have a few minutes to spare. It is now 7 P.M. and I have to go back to the shop and work till 11 P.M. Will."

And in a similar vein: "Dear Kiddo—Am working hard, have very little time to do anything else. I work from 8:30 to 6 at the International Harvester and from 8 to 10:30 at night. . . ."

Hard work or not, the Edwardians were immensely proud of the fact that they were getting on in the world. Lindsay, Ont., to Newmarket, May 10, 1909: "Hello, Miss Robertson! Lindsay is a great town. We have a fine office and all the staff are nice fellows. I am on the ledgers down here and like the job. D. M." (Young men, in addressing young ladies in those days, usually signed just their initials.)

Evidently some businessmen were thriving, as this brief punchy note from Winnipeg to Alexandria, Ont., 1909, tells us: "Still doing business. Did over $1,500 today. Love to you both. George."

Saskatoon, Sask., to Dobbinton, Ont., May 3, 1910: "Dear Father—I got work in Hills, Sask., at the door factory at $2 a day. I may get more soon. Gordon."

And from Lethbridge to Stratford: "Arrived in Lethbridge today, salary $125. Will write again soon."

One has to remember that Edwardian wages and business incomes have to be multiplied roughly by ten to arrive at an equivalent contemporary figure. A man making $125 a month would be earning about $15,000 a year in our terms.

It was the age of the small family store. In Amherst, Nova Scotia, Barkers Department Store, shown in this section, was evidently a real show place.

Nevertheless, by the turn of the century, Eaton's was already a fabulous enterprise and the largest retail organization in Canada. It had nine and one-half acres of floorspace in Toronto, a five-storey factory, and, depending on the season, from 2,200 to 2,900 employees. On July 17, 1905, Eaton's opened its Winnipeg store. Five floors made it the largest department store in the West.

Charles Woodward's first store was located at what is now Main and Georgia in Vancouver. In 1903, he built a new store at Hastings and Abbott and Woodward's was on its way.

Amherst, N.S., August 3, 1908: "There is a big rush on in this store all the time. Last night the windows were a dream. . . . Jennie."

A tempting display of distinctive home furnishings, from brass beds to grandfather clocks.

One of Timothy Eaton's zanier promotion schemes hung in the light-well of his Toronto store.

HARDWARE STOVES AND TINWARE.

BRUNSWICK ST., PENSE, SASK.

The cars were sold by Hugh McGillivray in Pense around 1914.

The Tiffany of Western Canada, Jackson Bros., Jewelers, Edmonton, Alta.

The Soft Sell

ADVERTISERS EARLY JUMPED on the postcard bandwagon. Sometimes advertisers published a series of related cards, and among the best of these are twelve splendid cards issued in 1910 by the American Telephone and Telegraph Company in the United States. Bell Canada had a close association with AT & T and it is probable that the cards were used in Canada as well. The scenes would suggest that they were aimed at the comfortably-situated families who were Bell customers.

The prize card in this section is one that shows postcards being printed in the Toronto plant of Warwick Bro's & Rutter. We cherish this card; there it is, all happening, and obviously in good volume, too!

Postcards usually sold to retailers at the wholesale price of two for 2 1/2¢ cents. The retailers' customers in turn bought them for two for 5 cents. There was a special deal for home-made cards, and there's one card in this selection carrying a Stedman Brothers of Brantford offer to print frame-view cards from a photo for less than half a cent each.

Whether of a humorous or prestigious nature, advertising cards were a choice medium for the Edwardian manufacturer who wanted to capture a customer's attention.

Toronto, March 2, 1906: "This is Warwick shop where the best Post Cards in Canada are printed." It's the Toronto plant of Warwick Bro's & Rutter.

Post Card
STAMP HERE
Domestic 1c.
Foreign 2c.
A GOOD PROPOSITION
We will reproduce any photo you may send us in this improved style of frame view card at the following exceptionally low prices :
500 Cards for $4.75
1000 Cards for $5.50
500 cards is the smallest quantity we can print. By large increase of facilities, we can positively guarantee shipment of cards in 10 days from receipt of photo.
Reprints: $4.00 for 500 ; $4.75 for 1000
With every order for local views for next month, we will give two large posters advertising that you have new views in stock.
STEDMAN BROS., Limited, Brantford

Mule Barometer
DIRECTIONS
HANG OUTSIDE
If Tail is dry—FAIR
If Tail is wet—RAIN
If Tail is swinging—WINDY
If Tail is wet and swinging—STORMY
If Tail is frozen—COLD
ON THE WORK DONE BY
15 Queen East, Near Victoria St.
Phone Main 4989

HOTEL
CARLS-RITE
YOU WILL FIND EVERYTHING HERE THAT THE WORDS COMFORT AND SATISFACTION IMPLY
THE HOUSE OF COMFORT
GEO. WRIGHT–E.M. CARROLL PROPS.
TORONTO, CANADA.
OUR FIELD FOR BUSINESS IS THE WORLD

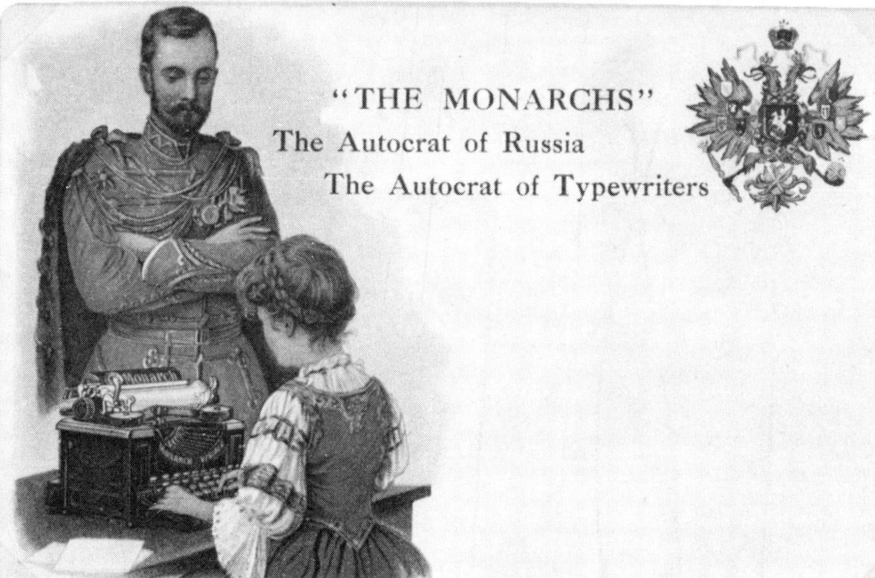
"THE MONARCHS"
The Autocrat of Russia
The Autocrat of Typewriters

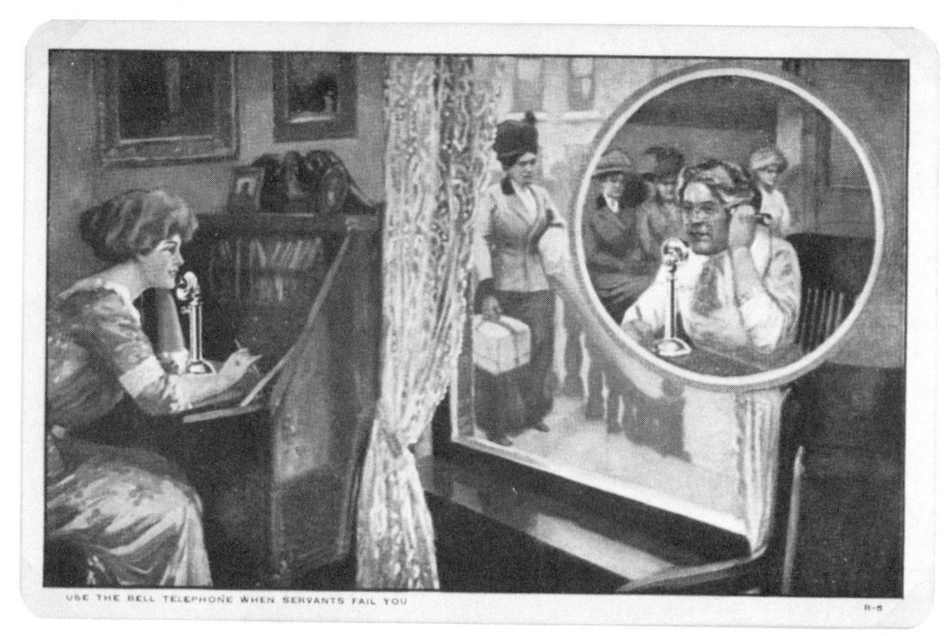

These 1910 Bell Telephone cards are part of a series of twelve that are rated among the best of the Edwardian advertising cards.

Golden Summers

THE EDWARDIANS had a passionate, enduring love affair with the summertime and holidays were precious to them. As much as American or occasional English tourists, Canadians took advantage of the many luxurious summer resorts across the country. The Pines at Digby, Nova Scotia, boasted a spectacular view. The Tadoussac on the Saguenay River was huge and splendid. The Royal Muskoka and the Wa Wa in the Muskoka area were household words in Canada and the United States. Banff Springs was immensely popular, and Glacier House, with the huge Columbia glacier as a backdrop, awed tourists. They wrote excited, happy messages to relatives and friends about their summer vacations.

Cedar Lodge Camp, New Tusket, N.S.: "There are four canoes and four rowboats and a guide to take one off on trips. One we took last week we walked right along in the freshly made footprints of a moose and saw the dam the beavers were making. . . ."

Blue Sea Lake, Que., September 9, 1909: "I am away up among the Gatineau Mountains 1000 feet above the sea level and 450 feet above Ottawa. Five of us are here for a couple of weeks and have a cute little cottage and do our own cooking. It is lovely. The scenery is grand and we are having a jolly time and are quite sporty fishing, etc. Love to all. Annie."

From Peterborough, Ont., to Toronto, July 22, 1909: "Dear Ella—I arrived here all right and am having a swell time. I have been out and had all the raspberries I could eat. I'll soon be as fat as you. Bertie."

Bobcaygeon, Ont., August 7, 1909: "Dear Anna—I am still away and it is very hot here. We nearly melt every day. I am learning to swim like a log and can go about two or three strokes. Ethel."

July 24, 1914: "Well here we are still in the wilds of Muskoka, of course having a grand time, boating, eating, and laughing with the emphasis on the eating. Just think of it, meat three times every day. I am no friend of meat so you see what a ravenous appetite we must have to eat meat so often. We have oranges every morning."

A cynic at Lake Rosseau in the Muskokas wrote: August 19, 1908: "This is the place where I am at, a way up near the moon and somewhat higher than ever. . . . The product of this place seems to be Air, Water, Giddy Young Women, Skunks. . . . The skunks make calls and leave their cards. Likewise the recipient leaves too."

Country people went to Toronto for holidays quite often. A message to Surrey House, Rockwood, Ont., August 18, 1913, reads: "I have not done a tap of work since I left home, eat, sleep, and have a good time."

Hanlan's Point, Toronto: "Dear Laura—Enjoyed just a lovely evening here, even if it looked like rain. Banana splits, ice cream, peanuts, oranges, pears, chocolates. Your friend Kate."

July 10, 1913: "Having a grand time and have met a bunch of people. Some classy gals, too."

From Port Colborne, Ont., to Toronto, August 1911: "We are safely here in a private house near the lake. It is very quiet. We are all out on the veranda writing cards. Marie."

Souris, Man., August 9, 1910: "Sunday morning we drove out in the country 4 miles and got a dishpan full of mushrooms. Weren't they good! Myrtle."

This on a card showing Capilano Canyon, B.C., September 6, 1909: "Doesn't this look beautiful? R. and I are having a lovely time. I hate to leave. . . . We walked up to the dam yesterday, about 6 miles altogether and down to the bridge this A.M. Lots of exercise!"

Is this an instance of faded summer's love? Brookman's Corners, N.S.: "Just a few lines to tell you you may as well give up all hope regarding it. I saw him out driving yesterday with one of S.'s fair ones and upon calling at a place last evening found him there basking in the smiles of others, though the scene was changed when I arrived. I felt you should know this so to act accordingly."

Or this? "Heard you had another fellow, but I don't believe it."

Then it was back home and back to work: "Dear friend — Arrived home safe and pretty tired. It is hard lines to settle down after such a wild time of it up there. Have you got over the effects of your holiday yet?"

"Dear Bea—Arrived home safe but minus one of my white shoes, but of course I wouldn't know I had been away if I didn't leave something. Hope all are well. Yours E. B."

Rockwood Park had twelve miles of driveways, a public garden, and a small zoological collection.

The Thousand Islands were dotted with some examples of extraordinary architecture—private castles and elaborately bedecked hotels.

In Front of the Grand Stand, Toronto Exhibition, Canada

"We are having a swell time, we took in everything this afternoon. We are sitting on the grandstand eating candy and pears. Will you have some?"

Jackson's Point, north of Toronto, was a very popular summer place in Edwardian days. It was described as "a pretty little village".

The CPR ran a moonlight excursion train from Winnipeg to Winnipeg Beach. It left at 5:00 P.M. and arrived back at midnight, and all for 50 cents.

Revelstoke, B.C., July 26, 1910: "Just a card to say I am feeling fine and having a good time. We are going to the coast on August 1. It will be quite a change for me. . . ."

"Dear Cousin Leopole—Many thanks for the pretty postcards. We are having fine weather. Yvonne is well, she is upstairs having a bath. Loretta."

Summer Sports

VERY RARELY IN THE POSTAL MESSAGES is there mention made of a book or a play. Instead there are endless messages about holidays, outdoor activities, and sports of all kinds. The Edwardians were physically active—it was part of their rural heritage—and sports, winter or summer, held a constant appeal for them. They were also spectatorial, displaying immense enthusiasm for the home-town teams.

Lacrosse was a rugged game and a popular one that suited the Edwardian temperament. If you carried a lacrosse stick during some of those years, you could ride free on Toronto streetcars. The west coast also had outstanding lacrosse teams. From Vancouver to Mitchell, Ont., June 5, 1911: "Dear Edith—Was to a big lacrosse game this afternoon. Vancouver and New Westminster. Our side (Vancouver) won 5 to 4 (Good). Over 8,000 people there from the tickets that was sold. Ever your friend, Lillian."

New Westminster's team, the Salmonbellies, did have their day, though. This is a message to Elbow, Sask., from Victoria, June 29, 1913: "Dear Frank and Grace—Goodbye. Am off for China in two days. Yesterday saw the world's championship lacrosse match between New Westminster and Vancouver. The former won 4 to 3. With love, your sister, Edith."

Baseball enjoyed continued popularity with kids and adults. A card from Toronto to Wiarton, June 17, 1909: "Nothing new here but baseball and that is old."

Another amusing message written by a youngster: "They don't strike me at all. I wear a baseball mask. Hope you will be able to come down and enjoy yourself. Tell Al he better stay home. She's gone."

There was a craze for canoeing and paddling. On summer weekends, the rivers near the larger cities would be crowded with canoes. From Winnipeg to Goderich, September 4, 1909: "Have been going to write for some time, but never had much news. Going on a long paddle to Morris, Manitoba, tomorrow and will get back Tuesday. Hope to have a good time if it is not too cold. Kindest regards to the family. Norma."

Ottawa to Eric, Ont., July 15, 1909: "We were canoeing on the Ottawa last night out at Rockcliffe Park, and Monday we were at Aylmer, 12 miles in 45 minutes by car and another day to Britannia and so forth."

Toronto to Niagara Falls, July 7, 1911: "Dear Mina and all—The girls are making bathing suits . . . love to all. Lina."

It is interesting to note how many women were sports-minded. From Bobcaygeon, Ont., to Toronto: "Dear Merd—I have beat you this summer at fishing. I caught 3 lunge in less than an hour. I'm having a great time. Hattie."

The adventuresome and energetic were drawn to the Rockies. From Banff, Alta.: "I went in bathing at the spring this morning, came back to the village and had our dinner and this afternoon climbed Tunnel Mountain about a mile straight above the town."

Summer afternoons and evenings were idled away with croquet, tennis was played on grass, and even small towns laid out cricket fields. Golf, horseracing, bowling, and mountain climbing should be added to the list, and Edwardians especially adored regattas.

North Hatley was a favourite summer spot with Montreal's Westmount residents.

Merry Bowlers, London, Canada
The Tecumseh Lacrosse Club, Hanlon's Point, Toronto.
"Thoney" on his way to first base. Opening game, Toronto, 1907
1907
"SUTTON BASEBALL CLUB"

Tennis was popular nationally. Many smaller communities maintained grass courts.

One of the best of all sports postcards. The tallest man is Ned Hanlan, the greatest rower of his time. Eddie Durnan and Lou Scholes were also outstanding scullers. Tom Longboat was the famous Indian runner who won the Boston Marathon in record time.

A bit of photo-journalism turns up on this card. These four girls survived a vicious storm on Lake Erie by paddling at least twelve miles to shore at Long Point.

"Dear Blackeyes—Am getting anxious to be home again. Don't let your papa scold me. Goodbye, Darling. E."

Joe Fortes, originally from Barbados, was a self-appointed and much-loved beach guard at English Bay in the early 1900s.

Bowen Island was Vancouver's pleasureland. Here, in 1909, the Sons of England gather for a picnic and races.

Caught off the Outer Harbour, Victoria, B. C.

Vancouver, B.C., July 10, 1905: "This is one I caught for you. You see I have changed my appearance some. I am 'Kingfish' here. C."

When Woollies Were Worn

BROWSING THROUGH WINTER SCENES of Canada in the Edwardian years, one can only conclude that the winters were severe, snow fell foot after foot, and the cold was relentless. Snow-clearing equipment was not sophisticated. Views of Montreal show men with shovels standing beside banks of snow that must be ten feet high. How they ever cleared a path is baffling, and of course, the answer is that often they did not. The snow hung around until spring when the city became a swamp.

From Park Hill, Ont., to St. Thomas, February 7, 1908: "There have been no trains out of here for two days now, and no mail from London for 3 days, so I would have heard from you I suppose. Snow, snow. It is awful. Love, Violet."

From Saskatoon, Sask., to Guelph, Ont., November 8, 1910: "Dear Lizzie—Are you still in the land of the living. . . . We have moved further West but can't escape the cold, it seems to be everywhere. Write soon. Lots of love. Cissie."

Neepawa, Man., to Castleton, Ont., March 29, 1909: "The snow out here is awful deep and the roads are a fright in some places. . . ."

Edmonton, Alta., to Nile, Ont., January 6, 1909: "We have it 46 below zero today, it's awful cold, I tell you."

From the Okanagan Valley, October 29, 1912: "Dear Sister and Girls—I have got started for Kelowna and am about 12 miles from midway. We started on the old stage and she broke down. I've got 107 miles to go by stage and it is snowing something fierce today. Will write when I get through and tell you what it is like. Don't come this way when you come. John."

London, Ont., to Barrie, April 7, 1909: "Terrible wind storm here. Several people injured and one school collapsed. Wind is still high so I am staying in. I'll be 'blowed' if I'd go out on a night like this."

And from Frankford, Ont., to Hoard's Station, March 2, 1913: "How does the weather ketch you? It was cold on Friday and the wind blew so hard yesterday pretty near upset me off the top of M.'s house. He isn't going to build his barn *this* fall."

Ch'Town
Mar. 30/06
Notice them working in the distance

Ice Boats at the "Capes"
This was the only means of communication between P.E. Island and the mainland for over two months this winter.

Northumberland Strait between Nova Scotia and Prince Edward Island could freeze over in the winter months. Iceboats—ordinary boats with double runners underneath and sails attached—carried passengers and baggage across the Strait until 1917.

Prince Street (Frosty Morning), Truro, N. S.

Blotty message on the reverse: "I presume you have heard all about it. P. wants you & Mr. Hunt to come up and stay. (Shoot this pen!) E. C. B."

Ice Cutting on the St. Lawrence.

Montreal Sweeper clearing Street Railway Track.

"I arrived home safe with a tooth-ache, sore toe and all my little parcels. Near froze to death walking home."

The Lakefield Preparatory School, A Country School for Young Boys – Lakefield, Ont

"It's just about cold enough down here to freeze people. If it soon does not get warm we will perish."

The awesome sight of Niagara Falls in winter helped make them a tourist attraction year round.

Winter Sports

EDWARDIANS WERE A RUGGED LOT, and eagerly took to winter sports. Children skated on ponds from an early age, and firemen often obliged by flooding outdoor rinks. Tobogganing was very popular, even on hilly streets where in winter there was no fear of traffic. Bobsleds were sometimes made by fastening a long plank to two ordinary runner sleighs, though there were very fancy ones such as the Foxy Quiller, shown in this section.

Men and women alike played hockey, and the women were just as aggressive as the men, although their long skirts must have been a handicap. Skiing caught on slowly as a sport after the turn of the century when the vice-regal set in Ottawa took it up. The Montreal Ski Club was founded in 1904, and the National Ski Association of Western Canada in 1912. Snowshoeing remained a sociable sport throughout the Edwardian era; people loved to tramp about in the bracing air.

This writer looks forward to winter in a message to Peterborough, Ont., from Cannington, December 11, 1909: "Good old winter has come again, soon be sleighing and skating. Good luck to you in your exams."

Toronto, February 3, 1909: "We were down to Moss Park Rink skating last night. Don't think it will be possible to go before Saturday but will hope for suitable weather then and look for you down early in the evening at Moss Park. We have promised to go there—we have two bands engaged already. Estelle."

Montreal: ". . . There will be 3 large sleighs, with 6 horses to each. We are going to Lumkins, that is West of the mountain, that means a drive around the mountain, then we will have light lunch at the church. It is the young men of the church who are giving this drive and Wednesday evening we'll go for a snowshoe tramp. Is that not tempting?"

Montreal, February 16, 1909: "The tobogganing is the best ever. Dorothy."

Toronto, February 16, 1912: "I told Willie he could use the bobsleighs if he would be careful of them and not let all the kids in the village have them, and told him he must put them back when he was done."

Haileybury, February 10, 1908: "Wish you were up here to see hockey. Games every night. 46 degrees below. This is the first mild day for near a month. Anna."

Then there was Montreal's famous ice palace and carnival: Montreal, January 25, 1909: "This will give you some idea of how the ice palace will appear. No doubt it will be a very beautiful sight when all lighted up at night. I suppose you will all be in the city during the carnival time? How many new postals have you in your album? I must have over 500."

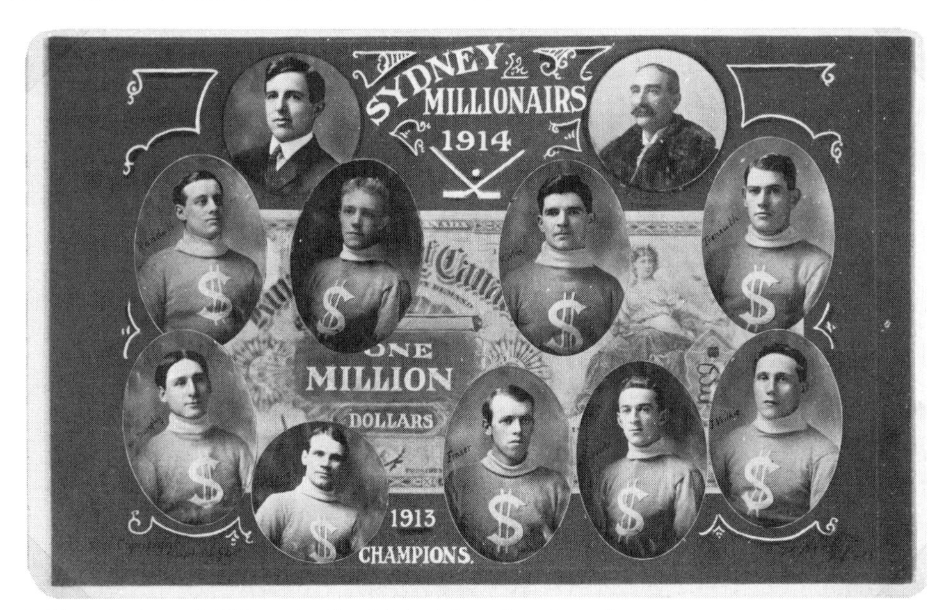

"The Sydney Millionairs" of Maritime hockey fame.

Notman of Montreal, the famous photographer, made this kind of photo-montage popular. It is a contrived rather than an actual scene.

Tobogganing, The Spill.

Canadian Sport Series. Hurdle Race on Snowshoes.

Ski-ing, Rockcliffe Park, Ottawa

“We are skating tonight. . . . Ask Ernie if he wishes me many falls.”

Romance on Wheels

"ROMANCE ON WHEELS" is an apt title. There is a direct link between "spooning" or "flirting" and transportation. It's a happy thought indeed that so prosaic and fundamentally useful an item as the wheel should at the same time be a gadget that allowed willing young ladies to be thrown into the arms of eager young men.

It was quite permissible to take a girl for a buggy ride or go bicycling with her or take her for a spin in your new auto— if she was daring enough to face speeds of up to 20 miles an hour. Easy transportation meant that romance had an opportunity to flourish away from fretful mothers and frowning fathers.

So this little section is dedicated to those marvelous caterers to Cupid, in an age when it wasn't all that easy to romance a girl: the buggy, the bicycle, and the first automobile.

WE HAD A SPLENDID RIDE.
463
A Stop for Refreshments.
Changing the sparking plug
16638
GEE WHIZ!...

April 18, 1907: "I'm writing this up in our cloakroom & it's rather dark (like Wednesday night), so excuse scribbling. . . ."

A Woman's Place

THE EDWARDIANS HAD AN AMBIVALENT ATTITUDE to women, and the female was cast in a multitude of roles. She was mother and, often in the West, an efficient housekeeper to a busy homesteader. She was a seductress who snatched away the joys of bachelorhood and replaced them with an ever-increasing brood of children and household responsibilities. She was idolized and put on a pedestal. She was pulled down from the pedestal and satirized as an old maid on the prowl for a man. In her new role as office secretary she was depicted consistently in postcard sketches as a delightful nuisance. She was seen sitting on the boss's lap or perched on a desk showing an ankle, or generally just disrupting office routine with her enchanting presence.

The woman as gossip is a common image. This message was sent to Grafton, N.S.: "Day before we left home, Mrs. A. called. . . . If she was looking for news, she got left, for I never mentioned any names, neither did she." Another comes from Winnipeg: "It certainly won't work. Clara is awfully sweet now because she is getting Jim, but just wait till the novelty wears off and she shows that temper of hers. Will anxiously await full particulars."

When a girl had a new fellow there was much excitement and kidding. From Atwood, Ont., to Coldwater, October 14, 1907: "Well, Elsie, this little berg is as wild as ever. Ethel has a new beau. Ask her if they have any frost up around Atwood. His name is Frost. Ha-ha."

This message is a good example of the good-natured but simple teasing that the Edwardians were addicted to, and it also includes the "ha-ha" that appears over and over again on cards bearing little jokes.

Men could be categorically unflattering about women, as on this card from Brockville to Hamilton, dated July 21, 1910: "We tied up at Howe's Island about 2 hours ago and two other fellows and self rode about 3 miles to this place. We've been walking up and down the streets looking like so many hobos. I haven't had a shave since I left Hamilton. Girls here are all fat."

Women in the West, because there were so few of them, could pick and choose as they liked, and it drove some of the country boys to distraction. This card was sent from Yellow Grass, Sask., to Avening, Ont., October 14, 1908: "Well, Alex, I guess you are having a big time down there now. I was down to Weyburn last Sunday. There is no nice girls up here, they turn their nose up about a foot. Jim."

We can't discuss Edwardian women without mentioning their huge hats, in particular the Merry Widow. These were festooned with all sorts of ornaments, ostrich feathers, even birds in full plumage. The hats were so heavy that women often suffered headaches after wearing them an hour, and postcard cartoons depict women sheltering 3 or 4 men under the wide brims of their hats.

Women's names had a fine, old fashioned ring to them. Lizzie was the most popular (never Elizabeth), followed closely by Amy, Agnes, Annie, Beulah, Carrie, Ella, Effie, Flo, Flora, Gertie, Hattie, Ina, Kate, Laura, Lucy, May, Maud, Nettie, and Sadie.

The drawings of Harrison Fisher and Charles Dana Gibson made the elegant American woman famous, and these cards were equally popular in Canada.

THE PANTALOON GIRL

First Harem Skirt in Winnipeg.

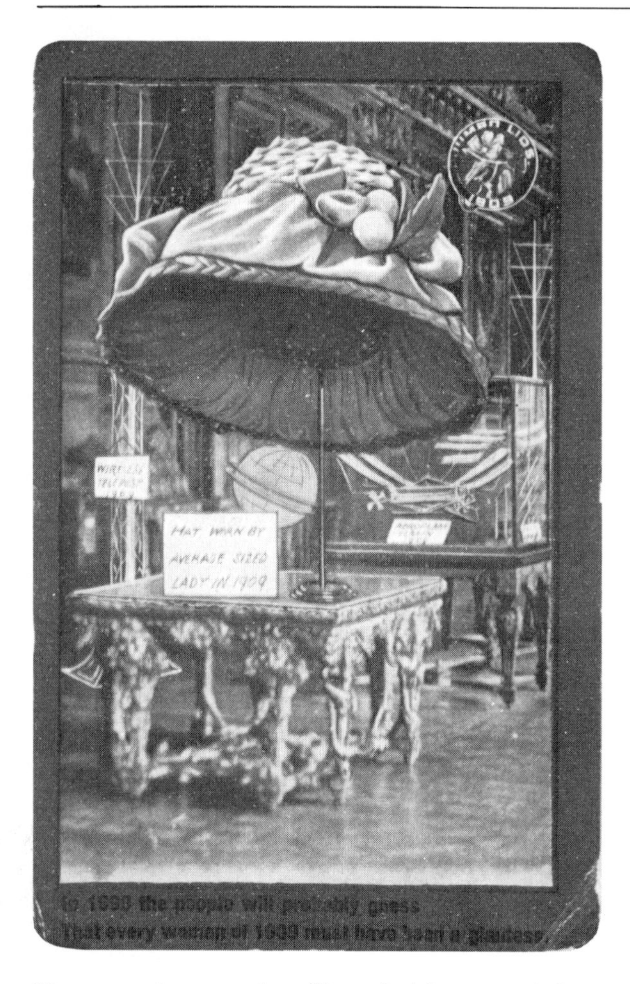

"In 1999 the people will probably guess / that every woman of 1909 must have been a giantess."

In the office, woman was usually portrayed as a seductress.

The message on the reverse is ironic: "Hello, Herb! Just a line, Laura is getting mad, she is waiting outside, so bye bye. Punch."

A Man's Politics

RURAL CANADA THRIVED ON POLITICS in the Edwardian years. Political discussions were an everyday occurrence, more lively and certainly more partisan than they are now.

Earl Rowe, former Lieutenant-Governor of Ontario and a man whose active participation in political life covered many decades, recalls clearly the importance of politics to the Edwardians: "It was a mark of citizenship in the community to be interested in politics and the church." Young people were warned to steer clear of "a man with no politics".

Elections and by-elections and the arrival of political dignitaries are noted frequently in postcard messages. This sparkling description comes from Victoria:

November 5, 1906: On the evening of the 26th, we went down to the wharf to see the reception of Premier McBride on his arrival by the Charmer. *He was driven away with three men, in a carriage draped with the Union Jack & surrounded by torch-bearers. The town was illuminated & as the procession went along, the blaze of torches & Bengal lights below & the strings of electric lights above was a pretty sight.*

They talked up their candidates' chances: Shallow Lake, Ont., July 11, 1913: "We are having a by-election on July 14;

watch and see us elect a Grit in North Grey." And they kept their fingers crossed: King, Ont., July 9, 1908: "I am living in hopes of hearing good returns from the polls tomorrow."

When Ottawa's fine old parliament buildings burned down in 1916, the House met temporarily in the Victoria Museum. Hence this message: Ottawa, April 5, 1916: "Have just returned from the parliamentary proceedings in the Victoria Museum. The liquor question was on and there were some fairly warm discussions."

The political cards in this section are intriguing. There are two political cards used in canvassing—identical, but for the parties they advertise. There is a card showing the Hon. Clifford Sifton, to whom Canada owes an enormous debt of gratitude; he was the one who swept the cobwebs out of the Department of the Interior, opened up the country, and filled the West with settlers.

There are several political cartoons, but most fascinating of all are a few cards dealing, in a kindly way, with the surge of American citizens in search of homesteads into the western provinces. Also, there is a card depicting the constant and substantial flow of British and American capital into Canada, a card that will have historical interest for Canadian nationalists.

JACK CANUCK—"I never buy a horse just by looking at his tail through the stable window."

Post Card.

JACK CANUCK — "Never mind the Tory Party. Just tell me of anything this particular bunch, that represents it, ever did for their country."

CANVASSER—"Well, I am not sure, but I think that when they were in power they crossed the jack-rabbit with the prairie hen so as to get a woolly egg that wouldn't freeze in the Northwest."

Sir Clifford Sifton (1861-1929), Laurier's Minister of the Interior between 1896 and 1905.

TO CANADA

For Investment in CANADA.

Serie No. 100

November 9, 1908: "I feel OK after the election. Three cheers for Laurier and a larger Canada. . . ."

An advertising promotion from Warwick Bro's & Rutter, Toronto: "This is a sample of our new election card, No. 441. Price per hundred, $1.25."

Unfurl the Flag

THE EDWARDIANS DISPLAYED IMPLICIT AND WHOLE-HEARTED LOYALTY to the Crown. Jean Gordon Gilchrist was a little girl at school at Tottenham, Ontario, when she heard of the death of the old Queen in 1901. She cried inconsolably until the teacher reassured her that there would be a new King and the Crown would continue as strong as ever. Later, as a woman, Jean Gilchrist summed up precisely the way Canadians felt about the Empire, about Canada, and about the new King:

As Canadians, we were intensely loyal to the British Empire and the British flag, but there was a growing feeling that we did not want to be colonized. We wanted to have our own Canadian independence, our own Canadian identity. I think the general feeling about King Edward was that he was a playboy and people rather liked that. He was genial and he made a lot of people very happy with his entertaining. They didn't take him too seriously but they liked him.

The story which best underlines our need to feel Canadian, and not subservient, is one related by Goldwin Smith, the famous author and journalist who lived at The Grange in Toronto. It is about the Governor General of that time, the Duke of Connaught. Just as I believe that people wore hats all the time during the Edwardian period (even to bed), so too do

I believe that there were at least three Dukes of Connaught, a real one and two impersonators, because he seems to show up everywhere. He travelled constantly, bestowing the vice-regal presence on villages, towns, and cities. On one occasion, on a hot summer's day, he got into a carriage and sat down beside the mayor of the community he was visiting. The mayor took off his hat. The Duke gracefully said, "Oh, you don't need to do that." The mayor fixed him with a beady eye and replied, "I took off my hat because my head was hot."

May 1910, Saskatoon, Sask.: "We have lost our good King. The post office as I write is all draped in black and purple."

The Duke of Connaught, then Governor General, and his splendid entourage, reviewing troops in Winnipeg in 1915.

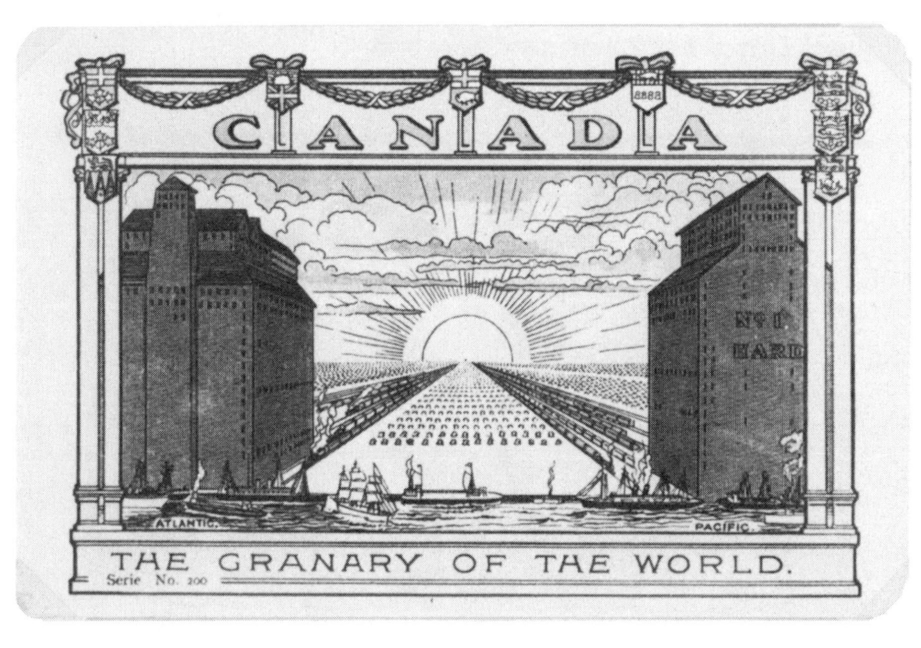

Spit and Polish

POMP AND CIRCUMSTANCE characterized the military camps and citadels of the day. Tournaments, drills, and the changing of the guard provided action and colour. Many a girl fell madly in love with a soldier and there was a great social life associated with the military. During the reign of King Edward VII, these extravagant military manoeuvres seemed very much a game. But the South African war was to leave many Canadians disillusioned — it was so far away and of no great concern to us and yet Canadian lives were lost in the Boer War and for what?

Military postcards, especially cavalry cards, give the dash and spirit of military life of those years. A message like this one is always a delight, because it provides such precise information: September 3, 1909: "We are having the best time of the year now. When it feels good to be alive to enjoy it. Very busy just now drilling in connection with the volunteers 5 nights per week for 6 weeks. Am enjoying it."

Another military message worth quoting is one by some simple-minded fellow with absolutely no sense of history. He was in Quebec at the time of the Tercentenary celebrations in 1908 and he sent a card home to Toronto, a card that reproduced the famous painting of the death of Wolfe on the Plains of Abraham. This is his comment: "I was over to the spot where Wolfe died, but it is nothing like this picture. I guess this was taken 300 years ago. From Sid."

An early and dressy military card, copyrighted 1898.

The Earl of Minto was Governor General from 1898 to 1904.

OFFICERS
OF
1860.
QUEEN'S OWN RIFLES OF CANADA,
TORONTO

Scottish Pipers
at Welland, Ont.

Canadian Military Series.
Mess time among the Men.

Officers, 15th Light Horse, Calgary, Alba.

Cavalry Manœuvres, Niagara Camp

Drill Hall, Vancouver, B.C.

Riders of the Plains

THE NORTH-WEST MOUNTED POLICE came into being in 1873 and was a no-nonsense force from the start. Some of its members became ranchers; having patrolled the ranch areas they had come to know the big ranchers and learned the game, and they took up spreads of their own.

The Edwardians, especially those on the prairies, respected and adored the mounties. The Red Coats kept an eye on early settlers and often helped them in times of distress. And school kids always got half a day holiday when the mountie visited the school.

The Royal North-West Mounted Police, as they were named in 1904, had their headquarters and barracks in Regina, and most of the postcards of the force in Edwardian days show a Regina location, although there are a few of the Calgary area and one very rare one—an absolutely fine card—that reads: "Foot Parade, NWM Police, Macleod, Alberta". In 1920, the force was re-named the Royal Canadian Mounted Police.

CHURCH PARADE R. N. W. M. P.

NORTH WEST MOUNTED POLICE

CHAMBERS
WCTU
R. N. W. M. P.
Moose Jaw
Canada.
Photo by Rice

Riding School at the Regina Barracks, R.N.W.M.P.

R. N. W. M. P. Barracks, Regina, Sask.

Mounted Police (Wagon and Escort) Western Canada, on line of Can. Pac. Ry.

Detachment of Police passing Officers' Quarters in Regina Barracks after exercise ride

Foot Parade, N. W. M. Police, Mac Leod, Alberta.

Novelties

An 1873 example of the many Victorian cards that had a plain back for messages.

POSTCARD MANUFACTURERS SHOWED GREAT INGENUITY in the variety of cards they turned out, more so abroad than in Canada, and well they might have—postcards in Edwardian days were profitable indeed. It wasn't just the variety of cards that were produced, it was the skill and imagination that went into the production of very unusual and odd cards.

There were celluloid cards, wooden cards, aluminum cards (they were sharp-edged and dangerous and were meant to be enclosed in envelopes), leather cards, fan cards, and pull-out cards. Homemade birch-bark cards were unique to Canada, and they stood up rather well in the mail and over the years. There were dainty book-mark cards often bearing excruciatingly tiny handwriting that tries the patience of the most devoted social historian.

The rarest of all novelty postcards are those on which there is a design of woven silk. Tricky to manufacture, they were not turned out in great numbers. Later, during the First World War, hand-embroidered cards were produced in France and were popular among soldiers who bought them to send home.

This card, unmarked on the back, is a precursor of the postcard. Such cards were sold on railway trains and elsewhere. They depict familiar scenes in eastern Canada.

These bookmark cards were sent through the mail like any other postcard.

"Grand Stand, Toronto Exhibition. (Seating 20,000 spectators.)"

MAIN STREET BRIDGE, MILTON, CANADA
CENTRAL PARK, GODERICH, CANADA
CUMBERLAND STREET, PORT ARTHUR ONT.
LUMBERING ON THE ASSINIBOINE

An elaborate fan card.

When pulled, this card shows a total of fourteen scenes.

Banish the Bar

In the four years from 1909 to 1912, the number of drunks arrested and charged in Canada rose by almost 75 per cent to 53,271, an increase that vastly outstripped the percentage increase in population. A well-organized and alarmed temperance movement had reached the conclusion that prohibition was the only answer. George Ross, the Liberal premier of Ontario, lost the 1905 election in part because even his own followers didn't think he was pushing temperance hard enough.

There are many cards of the time, usually of a mildly humorous nature, which depict a reeling drunk, and plenty of cards which show a man driving a water wagon with the slogan, "I'm on the water wagon now". There were even a few temperance cards, but most of them originated in the United States.

A little money bought a lot of booze in those days, and a publication titled *The Pioneer* reported on December 7, 1906, that Canadians were putting out "$10 per head per year for strong drink—or between $55 and $60 millions". Many a man took his pay, went to the nearest bar, and spent the lot. Affluent farmers lost their farms because of serious drinking problems.

In only a handful of cards is there a passing reference to drink. A card dated September 23, 1914, and mailed from Waterloo, Ont., to Valcartier, Que., reads: "Hello Fred. Had our opening young people's guild on Monday night, as usual a shortage of men, but had a nice time. Did anyone tell you we gave May a shower Monday night, had a great time, Harry sang and I think he must have been in a little happy spirits. Mabel."

From Cochrane, January 10, 1911: "Struck here last P.M. Of course I am pickled."

A man who must have been a commercial traveller sent brief three- or four-word greetings to his children in Toronto from all over the country. He outdid himself in Edmonton by telling them jokingly: "I was arrested at the carnival last night and put in the pen—the policeman told the magistrate I was charged with soda water and he fined me 25¢. Papa."

Souvenir Postal Card

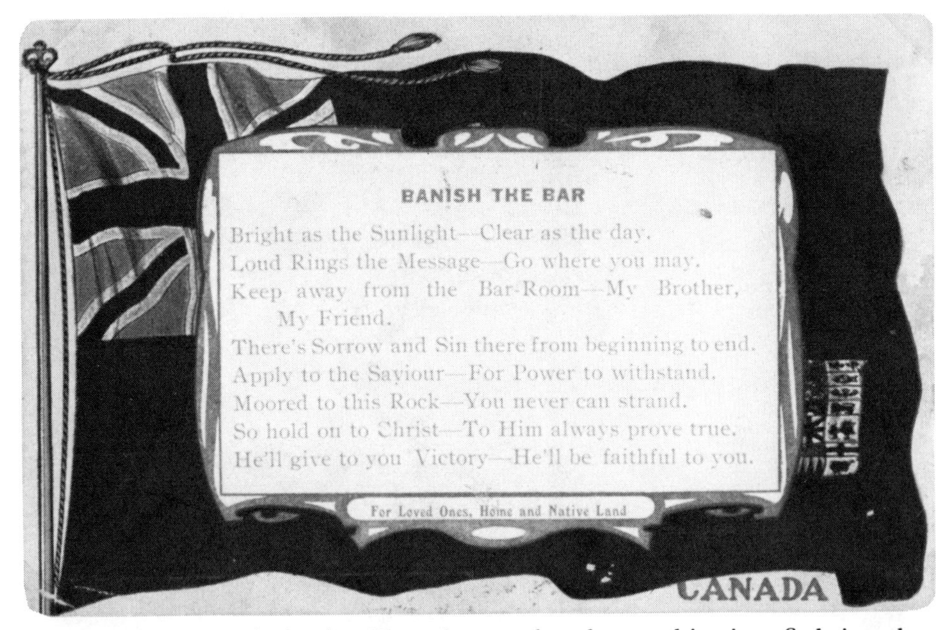

"I bought these to help the Church out, they have a big time fighting the liquor men here. Aunt Maggie."

We won't go home till morning,
Till daylight has appeared.
177.

A QUESTION OFTEN ASKED
In Renfrew
"NOW, JAMES HENRY—ANSWER ME!
HAVE YOU, OR HAVE YOU NOT, TOUCHED
STRONG DRINK TO-NIGHT?"

"I'M NO TEETOTALLER, YE KEN — BUT THIS
IS THE LAST 'SMALL SCOTCH' I'LL HAVE!"

Private Post Card

Innocent Laughter

THE EDWARDIANS had a rather countrified sense of humour. It was clean humour and we might regard some of it as rather lowbrow and simple. Nevertheless, some of the Edwardian funnies are endlessly amusing to modern audiences who especially enjoy the breezy off-the-cuff messages.

"Please tell me why it only costs 10¢ to get in the new botanical gardens while it costs $10 to get out. Is it that there are so many attractions that you can't help but spend many dollars, or that you have to pay that much in order to get out. Well I would stay there till they kicked me out. Ha-ha-ha."

"Let me know when you are coming to Toronto and I will engage the Royal Suite for you."

"Will be home on Wednesday if I don't get put in jail before that. Will try to escape the honour. I suppose you miss me."

"Well, I guess you will be pulling me over a broomstick when you get hold of me. . . ." "Over a broomstick" usually meant into marriage.

"Thought I would write to tell you that I am still on earth and not to Venus or Mars. . . ."

"You had better send Katie home soon or we will have to send a derrick down for her. Willie says he is yours for the asking. . . ."

"With me it is a continual round of pleasure up here, but we'll have to leave soon because the long greens are going so fast that I'm afraid I will be on the bum."

"Very hot today, 98 in the shade, sold 450 sodas, had a block of ice on my head all day."

"You should taste my cake—don't quite know what it was I used for flour, but never no more. However, they're still alive which is something. Maud."

"I am a new arrival in this city. Do you think it time for me to change my summer underwear?"

"My dear sisters—the reverse side of this card introduces for your careful inspection my landlord Mr. P. whose genial good nature, stomach-stuffing propensities and whose wonderful gift of song I have endeavoured to describe in former letters. He drives a bread wagon for a local baker here. Mine host is a bit of a wag with more of the fox than the dove in his make-up and on hearing Ethel offering to share her bed when either of you come a-visiting remarked, 'Don't ee bring either of your sisters to sleep with Ethel, her kicks like the devil, don't ee Ethel?' and to which the young lady referred to made no reply only a grin which to be sure is habitual here."

And the worst verse we have ever read:

Summer has came, the babbling birds and flowers,
Is sighing softly through the trees,
Tis tough that this poetic soul of ours,
Must work in weather such as these.

This is a leather card, (buckskin, in fact) and one that is often remembered today as a favourite of the period.

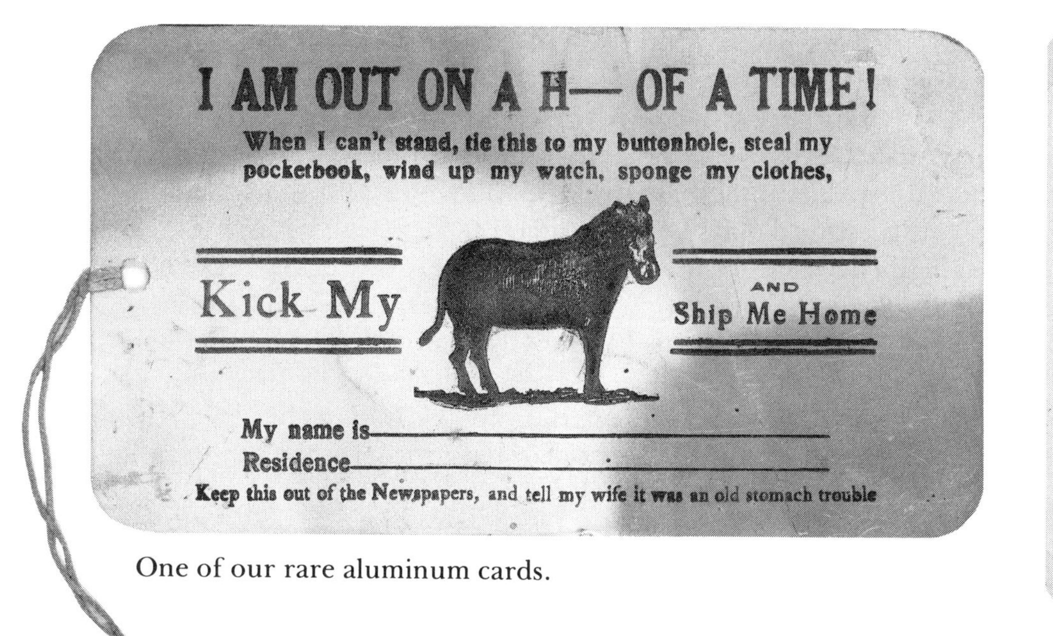

One of our rare aluminum cards.

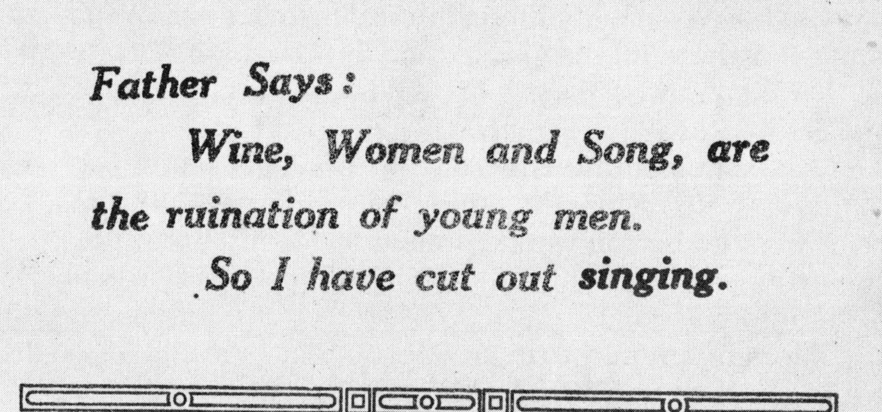

Maybe you'd like to
hear one of my
little speeches

I FINK I'LL BE AN ELEC-
TRICIAN WHEN I GROW
UP—AND SHOCK DE
GOILS.

Telephone Series
"I am on the telephone, but I am afraid
you will have some difficulty
in getting me just now."

Post Card

The Look of the People

PHOTOGRAPHY WAS VERY POPULAR and still enough of a novelty to excite Canadians. Kodak's slogan could not have been more appealing: "Point the camera, click the shutter, and Kodak with do the rest." Some enthusiasts have told us that they did their own developing in the back of the barn: "I did get some nice photos of places while out West but have not printed many yet, it takes up so much time. I will send you some after a while, lots of them were spoilt on account of the weather being so dull."

Studio photographers enjoyed a brisk business. Careful examination of some of the street scenes in this book reveals signs that read "Photographic Gallery", and Canadians trooped to the galleries to pose in ornate wicker chairs or against false backdrops of such scenes as Niagara Falls.

Homemade photos are frequently more engaging than the professional ones. A woman lounges in a hammock, a group gathers on a beach, or, in one case, a man holds over his shoulders two flour sacks, and in each is a young lady. In the background another woman holds her hands to her face in mock horror.

This message appears on the back of a card of a pleasingly plump and smiling woman: "Dear Folks—Just a reminder. Fat and sassy. Lovingly, Mae." Similar is this note from Grand Bend to Toronto: "You should see Daisy. She has developed an enormous appetite." Like King Edward VII, Canadians were good trenchermen.

In a complimentary vein, from Sherbrooke, Que., to a woman in Southampton, Ont., just married: "Sincerest congratulations and best wishes for a long and happy trip thru life. Tell R. C. that he has a jewel." And what is one to think of this message: "Dear Sister and Bro.—I suppose you heard that I have been fishing and caught a 'Pike'. Was married May 24 at 12. Walter."

The Edwardian character is evident in the best of these pictures—the sureness of family pride, the straightness of back and strength of character, and, above all, the enjoyment of life and sense of good fun: "By the looks of my pockets this morning, I must have had an awfully good time last night."

Dear Bessie:-
I am sending you one of my postals.
It is a fright, but only taken for fun one day I was over town shopping. Dont put it in your P.C. Album for if you do the others will be frightened and jump out. How are you getting along. Write me a letter. So long.
Florence.

"Many congratulations, dear Minnie. Very sorry it is not a little boy—but girls are alright."

"We are having a pleasant time and the boys are in the lake every day. Hope your hardwood floors are ready for Mike and me to have our fox-trot."

BOYS' BRASS BAND. PEMBROKE COMMUNITY MOVEMENT.

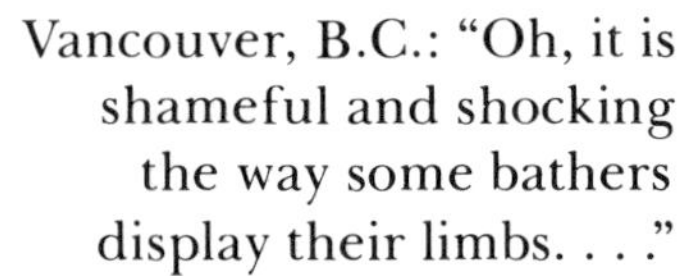
Vancouver, B.C.: "Oh, it is shameful and shocking the way some bathers display their limbs. . . ."

"We are going to have a picnic Queen's Day here. They make a holiday of it, so expect a grand time."

October 4, 1907: "Dear Folks—Fred S. is to be married this evening. Nell and I will stand up for them. We had just one day's notice. Hurrah!"

Mr and Mrs J.R. Ross champion
America
Ont.

An Octogenarian Party
Port Perry
Aug 6 /09

"1st Contingent of Youngstown, Alta." May 3, 1915: "Here is a bunch of boys that went from here. . . . There was quite a bunch killed a few days ago, the first ones marched got killed. I knew them well, fine boys. Oh, it is awful. . . ."